PRAYERS ANSWERED

PRAYING BOLDLY WHEN LIFE IS PAINFUL

CHRISTEN M. JESCHKE
AUTHOR OF RESCUE PRAYERS

Prayers Answered: Praying Boldly When Life Is Painful

PB ISBN: 978-1-969826-49-8
HB ISBN: 978-1-969826-50-4
E-Book ISBN: 978-1-969826-51-1

Published by Freiling Publishing
www.freilingagency.com

All glory to God, the true Author and Main Character of every story I tell.

To Jackelyn, Jillian, Jayla, Cadence, Britan, and Decker—I love you each so much.

"The Lord bless you and keep you; the Lord make his face shine on you and be gracious to you; the Lord turn his face toward you and give you peace." (Numbers 6:24–26, NIV)

Contents

"In the day when I cried out, You answered me, And made me bold with strength in my soul."

Psalm 138:3 (NKJV)

Introduction

For me, prayer has always been like breathing, a thought in, a prayer out. My inner dialogue is so intertwined with a constant heart-cry to God that it feels inseparable from who I am.

But what happens when prayer, like breathing, becomes painful? When every cry feels like a gasp that doesn't fill your lungs or a weight in your chest that makes it hard to whisper? How do you pray when it feels like you're reaching into a dark void for help, uncertain whether the God who sees will grasp your hand and fill your lungs again with His unfailing breath?

I have been there. Maybe you have too. There have been seasons when sorrow pressed so heavily that prayer felt less like breathing and more like suffocating, times when I longed to speak but couldn't spare the words. Moments when all I could manage were broken, desperate cries: "Help me, Lord." "Where are You?" "Please, God." Yet those were the very prayers God answered, not because they were eloquent or carefully formed, but because He is faithful. He heard my heartbroken pleas, and those cries moved the heart of a Father who loves us so dearly.

I was raised in a heritage of prayer. My grandparents were my greatest prayer warriors, their steady intercession covering me daily. My grandmother's prayers, in particular, shifted storms and altered circumstances, not because of her words but because of the power of the God she called upon. My parents prayed faithfully, too, as did many saints God wove into my life over the years. I stand here today not because of my strength, but because God, in His mercy, answered the prayers of those who carried me to Him. Time and again, He rescued me, not because of who prayed but because He is the God who hears.

I know my story isn't everyone's story. Perhaps prayer has never come naturally to you. Maybe you weren't raised in a home where people prayed, and talking to God feels awkward or intimidating. Or maybe you've tried to pray but felt like your words disappeared into silence. Maybe you're not even sure you want to talk to God at all because the pain you've walked through has left you wary, angry, or deeply disappointed.

You're not alone. Even a desperate cry like "God, help" is heard in Heaven, because God "bends down to listen" (Psalm 116:2, NLT).

Scripture makes this clear:

"Because he bends down to listen, I will pray as long as I have breath." — Psalm 116:2 (NLT)

The power of prayer has never been in our eloquence but in the One who hears.

This is why the *Rescue Prayers* series was born: to give voice to the cries we sometimes can not form when grief, anxiety, illness, or loss overwhelms us. Those prayers were written to help people lament honestly before God, to bring raw pain into His presence, and to discover how He works in power according to the unchanging nature of His character. This book, *Prayers Answered*, is about what comes after: learning to keep praying when life is still painful and discovering what it means to pray with bold confidence, daring to believe God is already at work. This is not a loud, showy boldness but the quiet confidence of children who know their Father welcomes them.

Courageous prayer doesn't bypass pain. It doesn't minimize it. True, faith-filled prayer rises from within the struggle, declaring, "Even here, God is greater." Bold prayer declares, "I can't, but You can." It lifts our eyes from the weight of the problem to the greatness of the One who silences storms with a word and breathes life into what was dying.

The veil has been torn. Through Jesus' finished work on the cross, we have direct access to God Himself.

"Therefore, brothers, since we have confidence to enter the holy places by the blood of Jesus..." — Hebrews 10:19 (ESV)

And because His Spirit dwells within us, we do not pray from our own weakness but from His strength. This is what gives us courage. This is what gives us hope.

Your pain does not disqualify you from praying with confidence. In fact, it may be the very place where God's presence meets you with the deepest power. Pain drives us to pursue the One who is able, and prayer places every burden into the Father's capable hands. Bring your lament, your questions, your desperation, and your longings into His presence. He already knows. He already cares. And He will meet you there.

My hope is that these pages will help you breathe again, not with shallow fragments of fear but with steady confidence that God is near. May you discover that even your weakest prayers can become bold when they rest in who God is, not in how you feel. May you find freedom to approach Him without hesitation, trusting that the same God who answered the prayers of generations past will answer yours today. He is faithful and able, and He will be glorified in the way He answers.

All the glory belongs to Him, always.

With audacious hope,

Christen M. Jeschke

A Rescue Prayer

Dear God,

Thank You that You are near to us in our pain and that not a single cry escapes Your notice. Thank You that even when words fail, You understand the ache of our hearts. As we begin this journey, teach us to pray with courage, not because we are strong but because You are.

Replace fear with unwavering faith, weakness with Your strength, and despair with the certainty of Your unfailing love. Let every reader sense the presence of the Holy Spirit and know beyond doubt that You hear and will answer.

In Jesus' name, Amen.

"You are the God who sees me."

Genesis 16:13 (NIV)

CHAPTER

One

When You Feel Unseen in Your Pain

It is hard to pray when life is painful. Pain can push us away from prayer and into places where we feel isolated, alone, and distant from God. Yet it is often in those moments when we feel unseen, invisible, and forgotten that God is closest, drawing near to remind us He has never turned away.

Scripture assures us that "The Lord is close to the brokenhearted and saves those who are crushed in spirit" (Psalm 34:18).

For some, pain is the raw ache of grief. For others, it is the unsettling buzz of anxiety, the depression that will not lift, the sting of betrayal, or the emptiness of loneliness. Pain pursues each of us differently, but that doesn't make it hurt less.

There is a particular loneliness that comes with pain. Even surrounded by people, you can feel like no one truly sees or understands your experience. How could they? That hidden isolation is its own kind of suffering. This is often where bold prayer is born, not in easy seasons, but in the places where we silently wonder if God has turned His face away.

For me, emotional and physical pain were intertwined: the deep wounds of enduring an abusive marriage were magnified as I struggled with immense physical pain from nerve damage to two muscles in my back. The nerve damage set off a ripple effect of muscular dysfunction and angry trigger points throughout my body, an issue compounded when an auto accident caused a slipped disc in my neck. As if this wasn't enough, I started having nearly constant migraines and a cascade of autoimmune issues that made my body feel as if it were burning from the inside out.

The nerve pain was the worst, a constant, searing fire like being branded without relief. My brain screamed so loudly with pain that it was nearly impossible to concentrate on anything else. It hurt just to exist. My very being became a constant cry of suffering. I didn't recognize my own life anymore.

The pain was concentrated in my neck and shoulder, yet it affected my entire body. My left shoulder winged awkwardly outward, muscles clamping and spasming in a desperate attempt to hold it in place. Moving my arm was difficult; lifting it was excruciating. Doctors prescribed a multitude of heavy-duty pain medications and muscle relaxers, including narcotics and opioids. None of them even touched the pain. Instead, they left me battling side effects, exhausted and discouraged, while still trapped in agony.

Sleep was nearly impossible, and the combination of pain and medications triggered autoimmune responses that led to massive fibromyalgia flare-ups and unrelenting fatigue. This wasn't the kind of weariness that a nap could fix. It was a bone-deep exhaustion that clung no matter how much I rested. I was constantly tired, and because of the overlapping issues, I was largely bedridden.

Still, I tried to push through. Caring for my small children quickly shifted from joy to a constant struggle, with every task feeling impossibly overwhelming. I refused to miss their school functions or activities, no matter how much I hurt. I kept showing up to my marriage and ministry, even if it meant paying for it in pain and exhaustion. Even with my best efforts, the truth was that life had diminished to mere survival. I couldn't even lift my arm to praise, and many days I had to discipline myself to choose joy or risk losing sight of God's goodness. Worship, once so natural, had become one more painful reminder of what I had lost. My new normal was both agonizing and isolating, as it seemed as though no one could understand what I was enduring.

Each visit to highly regarded physicians chipped away at my hope until there was none left. The verdict was in. There would be no cure. No relief. No end.

One Sunday at church, my adult Sunday School class gently asked about a recent doctor's appointment. Through tears, I choked out the broken words: "They said that I am going to be in constant pain for the rest of my life." With that confession, an overwhelming tide of discouragement crashed over me. *How could I live this way forever when I could barely make it through a single day?*

We all have moments that mark us, when a single sentence from someone seems to split life into a before and an after. It's in those moments that the question rises loudest: "Where is God, and why doesn't He see me?"

My whole life had been defined by strength, discipline, and endurance. As a former Division I collegiate athlete, I was no stranger to pushing through pain in pursuit of a championship. I knew how to grind through exhaustion and train my body to keep going when everything in me wanted to stop.

But this pain was different. It was not a pain to be conquered; it was a pain that conquered me daily. This wasn't just a disruptor; it was a destroyer, a relentless foe that broke me down physically, emotionally, and spiritually. With this pain, there was no winning.

Athletics had taught me that pain always had purpose, that on the other side of sore muscles and battered joints was a trophy, a championship, a victory. But this pain carried no promise of joy. It whispered only despair. It left me begging God for mercy: "Take this away, or take me Home."

And in the long nights, when my tears soaked the pillow, and my body trembled from pain-filled exhaustion, one desperate question rose again and again: "Dear God, do You even see me?" This is not a new question. Throughout Scripture, God's people have cried out from places of deep pain, asking if they had been forgotten (see Psalm 13:1).

That cry followed me into a Christian convention for moms, where I was swallowed in a sea of women wearing capri pants and buzzing with caffeine and freedom. There's a certain kind of energy when moms get away for a weekend without toddlers hanging off their legs or preschoolers melting down in the grocery store aisle. It's part freedom, part frenzy, and part sheer relief. You could practically feel the collective exhale in the room as women started their day in clothes not decorated with baby drool or sticky handprints.

Everywhere I looked, conversations hummed. Fresh coffee fueled animated discussions as friends reunited, laughter spilling across the tables. Moms savored meals they didn't have to cut into bite-sized pieces and finished entire sentences without someone needing a snack or a Band-Aid. The atmosphere was bright, loud, and brimming with connection.

But for me, the joy around me only made the isolation of my pain feel louder. Even in a crowded room, I felt utterly invisible, as though everyone else was thriving while I was stuck in survival.

And then came the words that simultaneously broke and healed me. The speaker's voice rose above the chatter: "There are women here who feel unseen, forgotten by God, hidden away in their private suffering. But I am here to tell you, God sees you."

Something fractured inside me. Tears poured out in a waterfall of grief and relief. Friends pressed in close, arms wrapping around me, prayers whispered over me. And in their embrace, I felt His. God saw me. He hadn't turned away. He met me right there in the middle of my pain with presence and compassion. The feelings that were too painful to voice, God heard and responded anyway.

That moment became a turning point. God showed me that He saw me in my suffering, and He surrounded me with friends who saw me too, friends who prayed over me, spoke life into me, and continue to lift me up in prayer even now. When I felt abandoned, God reminded me that I had never been alone: not in pain, not in grief, not in sadness, not in sorrow. He had always seen. He would always see. And what God revealed to me in that moment is something Scripture has declared all along: we are never unseen, even when we feel invisible.

Your story may not mirror mine, but the ache of pain is never insignificant. My pain may seem small compared to yours, or maybe the reverse feels true, but pain cannot be measured that way. Suffering can't be compared or quantified. Pain doesn't hurt less just because someone else may have it worse. It still devastates, disheartens, and destroys wherever it lands in life.

When pain lingers, it can feel like no one notices, not even God. If your heart hurts too much to pray, simply sit, breathe, and rest in this truth: God sees you. He sees your hurt, your sadness, and the weight of what you're carrying. Scripture shows us again and again that He draws near in our suffering, working in ways we cannot see to bring good out of what feels unbearable.

One of the clearest pictures of this truth is found in Genesis 16, in the story of a young servant girl named Hagar. Her life was not her own. Given into slavery, she had no say in where she lived, whom she served, or even what was done to her body. Her mistress, Sarai, handed her over to her husband Abram to conceive a child, and Hagar was given no choice in the matter. Sexually used, impregnated, and then despised by the very woman who had placed her in that position, Hagar bore shame and rejection she had never asked for.

Sarai's mistreatment became so severe that Hagar, pregnant, vulnerable, and without provision, fled into the wilderness. Alone in the barren desert, with no one who cared enough to follow, she was left to face her fear and despair. But she was not forgotten. Scripture tells us, "The angel of the Lord found Hagar near a spring in the desert; it was the spring that is beside the road to Shur" (Gen. 16:7, NIV). God didn't stumble upon her. He purposefully sought her out. The language of Genesis makes this clear, "The angel of the Lord found Hagar..." (Genesis 16:7), a reminder that God is not passive in our pain; He pursues us within it.

When you read Hagar's story, you may see pieces of your own. Maybe it isn't the desert, but you know what it feels like to run, to cry, to wonder if anyone notices. And into that very place, God steps near, not with indifference but with presence.

Alone, rejected, and carrying both shame and fear, Hagar was seen by the One who had never abandoned her. The Lord called her by name: "Hagar, servant of Sarai, where have you come from, and where are you going?" (Gen. 16:8, NIV). He already knew the answers, yet He invited her to voice the ache of her heart. This is the heart of prayer. It is not about informing God, but encountering Him. Abram and Sarai had only ever referred to her as a servant, but God gave her dignity by speaking her name. Hagar. Her very name means "foreigner" or "flight," a reflection of both her outsider status and her desperate escape into the wilderness. In naming her, it was as if God was saying, "I see you in your running. I see you in your suffering. I see you."

And God didn't just see; He gave her a promise. Her son would live. He would be named Ishmael, "God hears." And her future was not forgotten. Overwhelmed, Hagar declared, "You are the God who sees me" (Gen. 16:13, NIV). In her deepest abandonment, she encountered the deep love of a God who not only saw her pain but also refused to ignore it.

What is striking is this: God did not immediately remove her suffering. He met her in it. This is often how God works. He does not always bring immediate deliverance, but He offers undeniable presence. He gave her the strength to endure. He turned her wilderness into holy ground. And He entrusted this Egyptian servant girl, one with no voice in her own household, with the honor of giving Him a name: El Roi, the God who sees me.

We may not understand why God allows certain hardships to remain. But we can be certain of this: He does not abandon us in them. He is present. He sees. He hears. He carries us. Our wilderness places can become holy places, too, because He meets us there. Hagar's story tells us something unshakable about ours: we are never out of God's sight.

And when we question whether God really understands, we look to Jesus. God did not shield His own Son from suffering but instead allowed Him to endure betrayal, grief, agony, brutal pain, the savage destruction of His physical body, and even death. Jesus, the Man of Sorrows, acquainted with grief (Isa. 53:3, NIV), entered our pain so we would never suffer alone. Because of Him, we can be certain that God does not observe our suffering from a distance. He has entered it. And because He has entered it, we are never alone within it.

Hagar's encounter with God reminds us that prayer is not always polished words or triumphant declarations. Sometimes prayer looks like collapsing in exhaustion, running into the wilderness, or whispering questions through tears. Sometimes it is simply sitting in silence, resting in the arms of the God who sees. Scripture reminds us that even our wordless groans are understood by God (Romans 8:26). And yet, even there, He meets us. He bends down, calls us by name, and whispers, "You are not invisible. I see you."

This is the foundation of bold prayer: not that we are strong, but that He is faithful. Bold prayer is often born in the wilderness, in the places where we feel unseen, unheard, or forgotten, and dares to believe that God is present and working even when He does not remove the suffering.

When you lift your eyes in pain and dare to pray, even if all you can manage is a sigh, a groan, or a single desperate cry, you join a long line of people who discovered that God is not blind to suffering. He sees you. And because He sees you, you can pray with boldness, knowing that every cry reaches His heart because we now have direct access to Him through Christ.

Even when you feel unseen in your pain, God sees you.

A Rescue Prayer

Dear God,

I feel hidden in my hurt. It seems like no one truly understands what I'm carrying or how deeply this pain is affecting me. Even when I'm surrounded by others, I can feel invisible and alone. At times, I wonder if You have turned Your face away from me, or if my suffering doesn't matter. My heart is weary, and it feels easier to shut down than to hope again.

But Your Word reminds me that You are the God who sees. You saw Hagar in the wilderness and met her in her distress. You see every tear I cry and every ache I cannot put into words. You are El Roi—the God who sees me, who hears me, and who draws near. Thank You that I am not hidden from You and that Your presence reaches me even here.

So I come to You boldly, even when I feel unseen. Open my eyes to recognize Your nearness. Remind me that I am fully known, fully loved, and never forgotten. Lift my head and silence the lies that say I don't matter. Let this place become holy ground where I encounter You. I trust that You see me and that You are already at work.

In Jesus' name, I pray. Amen.

"The eyes of the Lord are on the righteous,
and his ears are attentive to their cry."

Psalm 34:15 (NIV)

CHAPTER

Two

When Your Cries Feel Unheard

The same God who sees you in your suffering also hears the pleas of your pain. I know this to be true because my own desperate cries for healing, once filled with hopelessness, were not ignored. God met me in the depths of my suffering and, over time, brought me into a place of restoration I never thought possible. What once felt like silence became the steady assurance that every tear, every sleepless night, every aching and heartbroken prayer had reached His heart. The God who sees is also the God who hears, and He is always at work, even when we cannot yet perceive it. This is the consistent testimony of Scripture. God hears, even when His response unfolds in ways we do not immediately recognize.

When your heart hurts, it may seem that God is far off. We may know in our minds that the same God who sees also hears us in our hurt, but we may not feel it in our hearts. In suffering, it can seem that our broken cries to be lifted out of darkness, grief, pain, anxiety, depression, harm, or brokenness go unheard, or worse, that our hurt doesn't matter to Him.

There is a unique ache in feeling unheard. When you cry out to God again and again, and there is no response, it can feel devastating. Calling on the Lord and hearing nothing in return feels like abandonment, and it can lead us to believe our prayers are wasted. When silence stretches on, it can seem easier to stop praying than to risk hoping again.

Yet Scripture reveals the opposite: God welcomes our lament. He knows the depths of our pain, so it is no surprise to Him when it pours out in torrents of raw, heartbroken prayers. When our emotions are laid bare before Him, God meets us not with reproach but with love, tenderness, and comfort, bringing peace even in the midst of pain.

If you doubt that God hears you and cannot see His goodness, pour out your pain to Him in prayer and expect Him to show you His presence. One thing I love about the Psalms is that they often begin as laments and then turn into declarations of God's faithfulness, as the one who cries out is reminded that His faithfulness never wavers.

But not every psalm resolves quickly. Some remain in the dark tension of unanswered questions. Psalm 88 is sometimes called the darkest psalm because it ends without resolution or joy. The psalmist cries out about sorrow, abandonment, and despair, ending with the words, "Darkness is my closest friend" (Ps. 88:18, NIV). This psalm is directed to God, even in its darkness, which means that even the most unresolved prayers are still spoken in faith. God allowed even this unresolved lament to become part of His Word, showing us that He welcomes our honest cries.

I find that stunning. God chose to include a prayer that ends without hope on the page, because even unresolved prayer is still prayer. The psalmist's words may finish in darkness, but the act of crying out at all is itself a declaration of hope, because it means faith has not given up. Prayers that feel unfinished are still heard by God.

I had read Psalm 88 many times before, but until recently I hadn't noticed its weight or grasped its significance. Looking back, though, it feels like the truest description of what I lived during my darkest season of pain. I lost hope and clothed myself in discouragement as each year that passed brought worsening pain and declining health. My prayers had no eloquence. They came out as groans, whispers, and sobs. Sometimes they were nothing more than tears that God alone could interpret. A heart without hope is a dangerous hurt. And yet, even then, my cries were heard.

In retrospect, I wish I had known the glory that was ahead, that there would be healing and hope restored. But when you are in the grip of grief or pain, it is hard to see beyond what you are experiencing. Well-meaning people offer familiar phrases like "Things will get better" or "God has a plan," but those words rarely bring reassurance when all you can see is the suffering surrounding you. What I needed wasn't platitudes. I needed presence. I needed to know that God was listening.

It is okay to pray the truth of your pain:

"Dear God, grief is breaking me..."

"Heavenly Father, I don't feel I can survive this depression..."

"Dear Jesus, this physical pain is more than I can bear..."

Prayers like these may feel too raw or too honest, but Scripture shows us they belong in God's presence. He does not silence us for speaking from the depths of our pain. He welcomes the cry. Scripture consistently shows that God does not reject honest lament but receives it as part of relationship with Him.

Psalm 116:1–2 says, "I love the Lord, for he heard my voice; he heard my cry for mercy. Because he turned his ear to me, I will call on him as long as I live" (NIV). God's posture toward us in our lament is not rejection but attentiveness. As Psalm 116 says, He "turned His ear" to us. He listens.

Even when your prayers feel unfinished or your faith feels fragile, He still hears. Psalm 88 may end in darkness, but it also reminds us that prayer itself is an act of defiance against despair. To pray at all is to say, "God, I believe You hear me, even when I cannot yet see Your answer."

Sometimes the most powerful prayers are only a few words: "Lord, help." "Jesus, please." "Father, I can't." Each one is enough. Each one is heard. God responds with compassion to the cries of His people. We are invited into a relationship where God hears and answers according to His will, not only in changed circumstances but in deeper nearness to Him and in the quiet formation that happens in His presence.

Returning to Hagar's story in Genesis gives us another glimpse of this truth. Years after she first encountered God as El Roi, the God who sees, she found herself once again in the wilderness, this time with her son, Ishmael. Cast out from Abraham's household with not much more than some food and a skin of water, she wandered until the provisions were gone. When the last drops were drained and the food was finished, her hope seemed to vanish with them.

I can almost picture the scene: the relentless desert sun beating down, the dry wind offering no relief, the heat shimmering across the sand. Hagar's lips cracked from thirst, her body weakened with exhaustion, her heart torn between the will to fight for her son and the despair of knowing she had nothing left to give. Ishmael, no longer a baby but barely a young man, grew faint with hunger and thirst. Certain that he was about to die, Hagar placed him under a bush for what she thought would be his final moments.

Unable to watch her child suffer, she turned her face away, sobbing in despair. But here is where the story shifts: Scripture tells us it was not Hagar's voice that Heaven highlighted; it was Ishmael's.

"God heard the boy crying" (Gen. 21:17, NIV).

That detail has always jumped out at me. God had already seen Hagar, and now Scripture highlights that He heard Ishmael. Even his very name means "God hears." This reminds us that God's hearing is not occasional. It is part of His nature. From birth, Ishmael's life carried the promise that his cries would not be ignored. When God named him, He was already speaking into this moment, declaring in advance that He had made provision. In His mercy, God ensured that Ishmael, the son of a pagan slave, would inherit the legacy of knowing a living God.

When Hagar first fled into the wilderness, Abram and Sarai had not yet received their new names. After her return, God established His covenant with them, renaming them Abraham and Sarah (Gen. 17:5, 15). Hagar returned in faith, trusting that the God who sees would protect her and her son. Her confidence was in the Lord, not in Abraham and Sarah's behavior.

It's important to note that Hagar's return to an unsafe environment is descriptive rather than prescriptive. This passage is not a call for you to return to an abusive situation. If you are in danger, God's Word affirms your need to flee to safety and not turn back.

The emphasis instead is that God had sent Hagar back to Abraham's household for a purpose. In that place of hardship, Ishmael was given the opportunity to witness Abraham's worship, calling on the name of the Lord, building altars, and receiving covenant promises. Though Abraham was flawed and human, Ishmael also saw how God patiently shaped him, growing his trust and obedience. Ishmael even bore in his own flesh the sign of that covenant through circumcision (Gen. 17:23–26). Again and again, his life reflected the reality of a God who hears and responds.

Through it all, Ishmael learned what it meant to see an imperfect father worship a perfect God. God did not immediately remove Hagar's suffering, but He remained present and provided within it. He used it to form Ishmael's knowledge of the one true God, so that when his own wilderness moment came, he knew exactly whom to cry out to.

And maybe that is the hope you need today. You may feel like your voice is lost in the silence, but Ishmael's story reminds us that God has always been attentive to the cries of His children. Even when it feels as though your prayers disappear into the wilderness, the same God who heard Ishmael still hears you.

God did not turn away. Instead, He spoke comfort: "Do not be afraid; God has heard the boy crying as he lies there" (Gen. 21:17, NIV). Then He opened Hagar's eyes to a well of water she had not seen before. What seemed like certain death became the doorway to new life.

And God's response didn't end with that single moment of rescue. Scripture continues, "God was with the boy as he grew up. He lived in the desert and became an archer" (Gen. 21:20, NIV). God's hearing was not temporary; it was enduring. His attentiveness became His presence. Ishmael's survival was not by accident; it was the evidence of a God who heard, who provided, and who remained.

Sometimes our wilderness seasons are not only about us; they are about what God is doing in those who come after us. The cries of our children, our families, and those who watch our faith do not go unnoticed. God hears them, just as surely as He hears you. And sometimes the very wilderness we long to escape becomes the place where future generations learn of the God who both sees and hears.

I have often wondered if my own children noticed the cries I poured out in the dark nights of pain. Perhaps what felt like weakness to me, my laments and desperate cries, was actually a testimony that their mother still reached for God when life was unbearable. The wilderness may break us down, but even there, God is planting something that is not wasted.

In the same way, Ishmael's cry in the desert became a moment of revelation: the God who saw his mother years before was the same God who now heard his voice. The legacy of El Roi, the God who sees, was joined with the legacy of the God who hears.

And that legacy continues today. Your cries matter not only because others may one day be strengthened by them, but because they matter to God right now. Even if no one else notices, He does. The God who hears you in your pain is the same God who can weave your cries into a testimony that reaches beyond you, in ways you may never see this side of eternity.

We may not understand why God allows certain hardships to remain. We may feel as though our prayers fall into silence. But we can be certain of this: He hears.

The psalmist assures us, "The eyes of the Lord are on the righteous, and his ears are attentive to their cry" (Ps. 34:15, NIV). Our cries matter to Him. Our whispers matter to Him. Our tears matter to Him.

And when we doubt whether He really understands, we look to Jesus. God did not shield His Son from cries of anguish. Jesus Himself prayed in agony in Gethsemane, "My soul is overwhelmed with sorrow to the point of death" (Matt. 26:38, NIV). And on the cross, He lifted His voice in lament, "My God, my God, why have You forsaken Me?" (Matt. 27:46, ESV).

The Son of God knows what it is to cry out and feel the weight of Heaven's silence. And yet His prayer was received, and through His suffering came our salvation. Because of Jesus, we can know with confidence that, even when we cannot explain our suffering, we can trust the One who hears us in it and walks with us through it.

Your suffering is never wasted as God works in all things according to His purposes. The very wilderness you long to escape may be the place where God is forming your faith, preparing you for freedom, and shaping a testimony that will echo beyond your own life.

Bold prayer, when your cries feel unheard, is choosing to declare by faith that God hears. It rests in the assurance that He hears because that is who He is, the God who listens to the cries of His children, and who has given you full access to His heart as His beloved child. Bold prayer dares to lift your voice when silence seems louder than answers. It believes your cries are never lost, and that God is always working even when we can't yet see it.

So let your heart be encouraged: every cry matters to Him. God sees every tear. Every prayer, even the laments, reaches His heart. You are not unheard. You are fully known, deeply loved, and continually listened to by the God who hears.

Even in your suffering, keep praying; God hears you.

A Rescue Prayer

Dear God,

I have cried out to You so many times that I feel empty. My prayers seem to echo back to me, and the silence feels heavy. I look at my circumstances and wonder if my words even matter or if my tears go unnoticed. It is hard to keep praying when answers feel delayed or absent. I do not want my heart to grow numb, but I am tired, discouraged, and afraid that my cries are falling into a void.

But You are the God who hears. You heard the boy crying in the wilderness. You listened to the psalmist whose prayer ended in darkness. You welcomed their lament and did not turn away. Your Word says that Your ears are attentive to Your people and that You listen when I call. Even Jesus cried out in anguish, and You received His prayer. Thank You that my honest prayers are not a burden to You.

So I come to You boldly, even when I feel unheard. Strengthen me to keep calling on Your name. Help me trust that every whisper and tear is heard and held by You. Move in what feels stuck and let me see that You are working. I believe You hear me, and I will keep praying.

In Jesus' name, I pray. Amen.

"Jesus wept."

John 11:35 (NIV)

CHAPTER *Three*

When You Can't See Past Your Grief

Grief is a pain that can feel unsurvivable. Loss knocks the breath from your lungs, and you wonder if you will ever breathe without hurting again. It reaches into the most personal places, robbing you of love, dreams, and future hopes. Even though loss is inevitable, it is not welcome or wanted. This kind of pain does not simply disappear. It leaves a lasting scar, a sudden halt to what should have continued: birthdays and anniversaries, ordinary adventures, shared texts or calls, inside jokes, plans penciled on calendars. Time tilts as you learn to recalibrate life without the person you love. The rebuilding can feel slow and tender as you adjust to a new normal you never wanted in the first place.

If that is where you are right now, Jesus weeps beside you. The empty chair at the table, the voicemail you keep replaying, the nursery that is too quiet, the clothes that carry their scent, the messages you reread, the conversations you wish you had, the house that feels still in all the wrong ways, none of this is small or simple. Grief can make the bright colors of life seem to fade into muted tones, where vibrancy vanishes, and painful reality remains. Whatever shape your grief takes, the ache of "Why, God?" and "Where were You?" echoes unbidden.

That moms' convention where God had shown me that He saw me when I felt alone, discouraged, and forgotten? A few years later, I returned with the same friends God had given me to gather around me in prayer and remind me that I was seen by God. The weekend had begun with joy and laughter, a welcome time of refreshment. Leaving one of the conference sessions, I noticed a missed call from my mom. Worried that something had happened as she watched my children, I played her voicemail, and my whole world flipped upside down. She had called to tell me that my cousin, Ryan, had been killed while serving with Marine Special Operations in Afghanistan. My measured and carefree walk out of the conference turned into a sobbing sprint as I ran back to my room and collapsed in tears, my lungs burning as the weight of the loss settled in. Pain poured out of my heart in a torrent of tears and aching cries.

My heart was shattered. Ryan was only three months older than I was, and we had grown up together. As little kids, he was my wedding dance partner, my playmate, my protector. As babies, we were dedicated to the Lord together. I grew up in a family of faith; he would not find his faith until adulthood.

With Ryan, everything had always been more fun. He was a mischievous child, the perfect balance of impishness and absolute charm. He was brilliantly curious. If he knew I cared about a subject, he would research it so we could discuss it. Usually, that subject was gymnastics, my childhood passion. He would read books on it, learn the names of skills, and ask me question after question. While he had a reputation for roughhousing with other cousins, Ryan always treated me like a princess, and I admired him endlessly for it. He was my real-life hero, and losing him pierced me deeper than anything I knew how to express.

Ryan was made to be a Marine. Many generations of our family had served in the Marine Corps, so it was no surprise when he decided to join. It seemed a natural fit, like a calling carved specifically for him. While we knew that ultimate sacrifice was often the high cost of service, we never wanted to contemplate that our Ryan could be taken.

The news of Ryan's death in a highly publicized green-on-blue attack that murdered three US soldiers ripped our hearts wide open. He was loved by so many and deeply admired. His death was shockingly sudden and deeply devastating. *Why, God? Where are You in this?*

As headlines circulated and news anchors relayed the sparse details, a strange dissonance settled over me. The news media was quick to report the facts of the attack; yet the often incorrect and coldly clinical explanations could not capture the truth of who these young men really were. They were sons and brothers, husbands and fathers, friends and teammates. They had laughed, dreamed, sacrificed, and imprinted memories on every heart fortunate enough to know them. What the world saw were brief summaries. What we lost were whole lives, rich with stories and love.

I felt so much pain at his loss that I could not believe the world continued to function around me. It felt wrong that traffic kept moving, people still chatted in coffee shops, and the sun continued to rise as if nothing had changed. As I watched strangers go about their daily lives, I wanted to stop them and plead for them to understand that everything was different now. Ryan was gone, and the world should have paused to notice.

Although we may never have answers this side of glory for why God allowed Ryan to be taken from this earth so soon, we began to see that even in tragedy, God had not stepped away. In small and surprising ways, He showed us that our pain was not invisible to Him and that He was not wasting what we could not understand.

For me, God was present in my closest friends as they stayed with me through those first terrible days. They hugged me, held me, cried with me, and let me grieve through both sobbing and laughter as I recounted some of Ryan's hilarious antics.

God was there in a Spirit-given boldness to witness to those around me about the hope I have: the assurance that Ryan is with the Lord, grounded in his confession that Jesus is Lord and in the promise that, in Christ, death does not get the last word.

God was also present in a quiet reminder that what we could see was not the whole story. It felt like staring at a single ugly quilt square, colors that clash and stitching that seems harsh, a piece that looks nothing like beauty. But a master quilter does not judge the pattern by one square. He sets each piece into a larger design where the dark blocks give depth to the light. God takes even the torn and jagged pieces and sets them into a larger design, where what looks harsh up close can, in time, become part of unexpected beauty. What sat in our hands was painful and not reflective of God's desire for a broken world, but it was not the pattern's end.

In the days that followed, several of us received personal comforts, small mercies that reassured our hearts that Ryan was held by a God whose love is deeper than we can grasp. Some had comforting dreams, others found a timely verse or an unexpected calm, each one a quiet stitch of kindness in the middle of grief.

One testimony, though, touched us all. When my Aunt Carolyn, Ryan's mom, received the news that he had been killed, she grieved alone in a quiet house, pouring out sobs and groanings too deep for words. In that anguish, she sensed the Lord meet her with a vivid mercy, a picture of Ryan with the simple assurance, "Mom, I'm okay." Peace washed over her in a way she could not explain, like a steady hand placing that jagged quilt square into something truer than sorrow.

Weeks later, I sat beside her, cradling Ryan's newborn nephew, and she told me through tears what that moment set in motion. A faith she had kept on a shelf for more than forty years was lifted down and opened. She surrendered her life to Christ and was baptized soon after. We all observed the same thing: if Ryan could have chosen to lay down his life so that his mom would one day join him in heaven, he would have done so without hesitation. I don't believe God "needed" Ryan's death to reach her, and I don't pretend this one story explains our loss. But in that testimony, without claiming to fully understand His purposes, we caught a glimpse of the larger quilt God is weaving, as a beautiful piece was added when a life was surrendered to Christ. We still hold only one square in our grief, yet that bright thread of redemption runs through it, a sign that even here, God has not abandoned us.

You may not be ready to see any quilt pattern at all in your own story. Maybe all you can see is the jagged edge in your hands and the empty space where your loved one should be. That is okay. God is not in a hurry for you to move on or declare false silver linings. He is willing to sit with you in the unfinished places.

Maybe you cannot see any good in your grief story. Maybe all you can feel is darkness, weeping, and sorrow. Cry out to Jesus. He will meet you there, too. He is steady when everything feels uncertain, your rock when the ground shifts, your refuge when the waves rise. He understands your sorrow, and He weeps too. Scripture describes Him as our refuge and strength, an ever-present help in trouble (Psalm 46:1).

Maybe your grief shows up in the quiet places of your life, the mornings that feel heavier than they used to, the tasks that take twice the energy they once required. Maybe it's the nights when sleep slips through your fingers, or the way your heart tightens when you realize you're stepping into another day without them. Perhaps you are caring for others with a strength you don't feel, or wrestling with questions that have no easy answers. Maybe certain dates, songs, seasons, or routines now carry an ache you never expected to feel. Whatever shape it takes, Jesus sees the toll it takes on your body, your mind, your spirit. He sees the moments no one else notices, and He meets you in all of them with compassion that does not grow tired.

When all you can see is the painful, broken square in your hands, prayer becomes the way you place that piece into His. Even your questions and accusations, "*Why, Lord?*" "*Where were You?*" can become part of that prayer. Scripture gives us a window into this in the story of Lazarus. Jesus' dear friends, Martha and Mary, lived with their brother in Bethany. When Lazarus fell gravely ill, the sisters sent a simple message: "Lord, the one You love is sick." They knew that if Jesus came, Lazarus would be healed. Still, Jesus did not leave at once. He waited two days with a purpose His friends could not yet see. As John records that this delay was for God's glory (John 11:6, 11:4). By the time Jesus arrived, Lazarus had been in the tomb four days. Hope felt ridiculously foolish.

Martha went to meet Jesus on the road, grief and faith colliding, and said plainly, "Lord, if You had been here, my brother would not have died." She did not soften the edge of her sorrow, and Jesus did not rebuke her honesty. Maybe you have said something similar: "Lord, if You had been here, this wouldn't have happened." He can bear that sentence from your lips, too. Jesus lifted her gaze to something larger, Himself. "Your brother will rise again," He said. Martha reached for the truth she knew, the resurrection at the last day, but Jesus brought that future hope into the present: "I am the resurrection and the life." (John 11:25) Not a distant event, but a living Person standing before her. He claimed to be the source of life in all things, the One who holds authority over death and who gives life now to all who trust Him.

Mary came later, fell at His feet, and spoke the very same words Martha had used. Her tears undid the crowd, and they moved Jesus, too. The text says He was "deeply moved in spirit and troubled" (John 11:33), revealing both compassion and righteous grief. He asked where they had laid Lazarus, went with them to the tomb, and there He wept. (John 11:35) The One who knows the end of the story does not hurry past the ache of the middle. He stands with us in our pain and lets His own tears fall. If Jesus did not shame their tears, He will not shame yours.

Then He told them to roll away the stone. Even faithful Martha hesitated, knowing decay and stench had set in. She believed Jesus could have prevented the loss if He had been there, but four days had passed since His death. What good would reopening the tomb do? Would it only reopen a wound and raise false hope? Yet Jesus pressed the question of trust. If they believed, they would see the glory of God. The stone was moved. He prayed aloud so those watching would know the Father hears the Son. Then He cried out, "Lazarus, come out." (John 11:43) Life recognized its Lord. Lazarus stepped into daylight, still wrapped in grave clothes, and Jesus told the community to unbind him. Even miracles invite help, and hope loosens what still clings.

Why does this matter for how we pray when grief crushes us? Because this scene teaches us what bold prayer really is. Bold prayer does not pretend the tomb is empty; it brings Jesus to the tomb. It speaks honestly, as the sisters did, "Lord, if You had been here," and then holds fast to who He is, "I am the resurrection and the life." Bold prayer dares to ask for what only God can do, while trusting His heart in the waiting. It takes the next obedient step, rolling away the stone we can move, while leaving the raising to Him. It welcomes the people God sends to help unwrap what sorrow has bound. It prays from the middle of the story, not only the ending, because we know the Author is at work even when we cannot see the final page.

Bold prayer in grief might sound like, "Jesus, I don't understand why You didn't stop this, but I am asking You to sit with me in this pain and show me that You are here," or,

"Lord, I cannot imagine anything good coming from this, but I place this broken piece in Your hands anyway."

Bold prayer lives in two directions at once, honest about the sorrow of today and certain of the joy that is coming. Jesus stands with us at the tomb, and He will one day bring resurrection and restoration, as Scripture promises (John 5:28–29; Revelation 21:4). That future promise doesn't hurry our grief along; it steadies our hearts as we walk through it. We ask for help today, confident that the story God is writing ends in restoration, not loss.

A Rescue Prayer

Dear God,

My heart is shattered, and grief feels overwhelming. I miss the one I love, and the empty spaces in my life are too loud to ignore. Ordinary moments have become painful reminders of what will never be. I do not know how to keep going when it hurts this much. I cannot see beyond the ache, and even simple tasks feel heavy.

But You are the God who meets me in my sorrow. You wept at Lazarus's tomb, even knowing resurrection was coming. You are close to the brokenhearted and save those who are crushed in spirit. You do not rush my grief or shame my tears. You are the resurrection and the life, and death does not have the final word. Thank You that my pain is safe with You.

So I place this broken part of my heart in Your hands. Give me faith to believe You are still good, even now. Sit with me in the sorrow and remind me that You are near. Help me trust You with what I cannot understand. Lift my eyes, little by little, to see that You are still at work. Hold my grief within Your promise of resurrection, and give me courage to keep praying.

In Jesus' name, I pray. Amen.

"Trust in the Lord with all your heart and lean not on your own understanding; in all your ways submit to him, and he will make your paths straight."

Proverbs 3:5–6 (NIV)

CHAPTER

Four

When It Is Hard to Trust

Trusting God when life is painful is hard. I know that's a sentence we're not supposed to say out loud, but it's true. It's easy to trust God when life feels good: when your body is healthy, grief feels distant, joy surrounds you, your relationships are thriving, and prayers seem to be answered just the way you hoped. But suffering changes everything. Trust begins to waver when things get difficult. In those moments, doubt seeps in quietly, and you begin to wonder: If God really loves me, why hasn't He taken this away? Why would He let me suffer like this? Can I really trust Him to keep His promises when He's allowing me to stay in this pain? Where are You, God, and are You even good? Instead of resting in His peace, you feel caught between what you know of God's goodness and what your pain seems to prove. Trust isn't certainty about outcomes; it's confidence in God's character.

Throughout my life, I've seen God move seemingly immovable mountains, and yet I still struggle to trust. I've watched Him provide in miraculous ways, answer prayers I thought were impossible, and carry me through seasons I never imagined surviving. You would think this would make my trust unshakable, but when new challenges arise, doubt is never far behind. Obviously, my faith is far from perfect, which only makes me more grateful that I serve a God who is perfectly faithful.

Maybe you can relate: you know God has worked in your past, but you're unsure whether you can trust Him with your future. If that's you, you're not alone. There is a real tension in wrestling with trust, even as we cling to faith. Or maybe you don't yet know God at all. You haven't tasted and seen His goodness, so you wonder if the stories of His love are true for you. You question. You doubt. You cry. You mourn. You plead. And you wonder: *Will God come through for me? Does He see how desperate I am? Does God even care?*

Trust, it turns out, is not a one-time decision you settle forever. It is a daily surrender, a certainty formed through submission and obedience, choosing to rely on God even when you cannot see the outcome. Trust is a choice made again and again, especially when life hurts and the help you long for still feels far away, and it is strengthened by remembering where God has helped you before.

For many years, I lived in so much physical and personal pain that it felt like I was at the bottom of a hole I couldn't climb out of. The light of God's goodness was still there, but it felt far beyond my reach. Every day was endlessly hard. My physical pain grew progressively worse, and I had no real hope for healing. It's not that I didn't seek healing; I did. If someone suggested a treatment, I tried it. If there was a specialist with a promising solution, I pursued it. I put my hope in doctors who let me down again and again. I took medications that never touched the pain. I exhausted myself with my own efforts to find healing. I trusted every human solution that I could find, and they all failed me. At the same time, I was losing trust in the only One who had never failed me. Seeking solutions was not wrong, but shifting my eyes away from the true source of healing was a mistake.

It wasn't that I stopped believing in God. I knew He was real. But as disappointment piled up, I doubted His power to heal me, and even whether He loved me enough to take my pain away. My prayers withered into small, cautious words. I prayed, but without expectation. I asked, but secretly assumed the answer would be "no." I still sought Him, but I also settled into the lie that life could never be truly joyful again. Deep down, I had convinced myself His healing and kindness were reserved for others, not for me. This devastated me.

And it wasn't just physical pain. My marriage grew more destructive with each passing year, and the eggshells I had tiptoed across for so long finally gave way under the weight of my spouse's anger and addiction. I had long tried to shield my children and myself through attempts at perfection, catering to my husband's moods and demands, supporting his work and hobbies, keeping an obsessively clean house, staying fit, caring for my appearance, preparing hot meals, volunteering in ministry, teaching Sunday school, and striving to be the perfect wife and mother. I thought if I could just be enough, maybe it would keep everything safe and calm for my children. But the harder I tried, the more fragile everything became. No matter what I did, I could never be enough.

In chasing perfection, I wasn't only trying to protect my children; I was also relying on myself instead of trusting the God who had always been faithful.

Perfectionism is born of pride, and pride is trusting in yourself instead of in God. Pride convinced me that if I could just be good enough, loving enough, pretty enough, supportive enough, kind enough, capable enough, I could somehow manage my spouse's moods and excuse his covenant-breaking behavior. I never paused to admit that his brokenness was beyond my ability to repair. Instead, I chased an impossible standard that left me weary. No matter how much I strove, I could never be enough to fix what was broken.

For so many years, I leaned on perfectionism to cover and control the brokenness that existed behind closed doors. And for a time, I thought it worked, a fragile balance at best. But everything changed when pain came crashing in. What I had managed in health, I could no longer manage in weakness. In that season, it was as if God stripped away the idol of self-reliance to expose the deeper problems. I had been pridefully trusting in myself to hold everything together: my marriage, my home, my image, even my faith.

When pain wrecked me, my striving collapsed. And with it, the truth surfaced: I wasn't doubting God's existence; I was doubting His heart. I had trusted Him only as long as He gave me the outcomes I wanted. My faith wasn't anchored in who He is but in what I thought He should do for me. When He didn't move on my timeline or in the way I expected, my trust faltered. I wanted His power, but I didn't rest in His character. In God's faithfulness, He would rebuild my trust by letting everything I falsely trusted in fall apart.

The difficult parts of my story have served a purpose, but that did not make them hurt less. One of the hardest seasons, and also one in which I sensed God's nearness most, was when my marriage ended. Divorce is the death of a dream, the funeral of the future you imagined when you joined your life to someone else. For me, it was the sober acknowledgment of a covenant repeatedly broken and a pattern of harm I could no longer deny. I realized I was gripping the institution of marriage more tightly than the truth; that was idolatry, not faithfulness. Naming that truth was a deep grief. When God released me from my destructive marriage, I naïvely thought safety would follow; instead, filing for divorce brought challenges I did not anticipate, and the danger for my children and me only increased. It was a scary time in which everything I held tightly seemed to be stripped away as the life we knew shattered around us. Any stability we had relied on disappeared. Everything grew worse before anything grew better.

That season also revealed how I had started to confuse God with the people who had failed me. Doctors failed to fix my pain, so I wondered if He would too. My spouse broke trust, so I questioned whether God's promises could truly be counted on. Even my own body betrayed me, breaking down under relentless pain until I could no longer rely on my own strength. The rejection I carried from others made me view God through a distorted lens, as if He, too, might eventually let me down. I was judging His character by human patterns, not by His Word.

But God is not like people, and He is not like my frail body. He does not fail. He does not abandon, as Scripture assures us that He will never leave nor forsake His people (Hebrews 13:5). He does not grow weary of me. His promises do not wilt like human words; they are steady, unshakable, and true. He is the Faithful One, the Rock that cannot be moved, the Healer who binds up wounds, the Father who never leaves His children, the Shepherd who carries the weak, and the Redeemer who restores what is broken. My "never enough" rests in His "always enough."

That undoing, painful as it was, became a strange kind of mercy, because when self-reliance and false views of God finally crumble, the only place left to stand is on who He really is. And who He is is enough. If God is this faithful and strong, then our honest sorrow is safe with Him. Lament is how trust speaks in pain.

Lament is not weakness or faithlessness. It is one of the purest expressions of trust. To lament is to turn to God with our pain rather than turning away from Him. Scripture is filled with cries of lament: "How long, O Lord," "Why have you rejected me," "Has God forgotten to be gracious" (Ps. 13:1; Ps. 42:9; Ps. 77:9, NIV). These are not sanitized prayers tied up neatly with resolution; they are gut-level honesty, preserved in God's Word to show us that He welcomes our anguish. When you pour out your hurt to Him, you are not failing at faith; you are practicing it.

What sets biblical lament apart from despair is the turn it takes. The psalmists do not stop with grief; they move toward

God's character. In Psalm 13, David begins with, "How long, Lord, Will you forget me forever?" yet the psalm ends with, "But I trust in your unfailing love; my heart rejoices in your salvation" (Ps. 13:1, 5, NIV). His circumstances didn't change in those six verses, but his heart did. He chose to root himself in what he knew of God's character, even when he couldn't see the outcome. Lament becomes the bridge between raw pain and renewed trust.

We also see this in Job, whose life was shattered in ways few of us can imagine. He lost his children, his health, his wealth, his reputation, stripped away in a whirlwind of suffering. Job cried out bitterly, accusing, questioning, lamenting: "I cry out to you, God, but you do not answer; I stand up, but you merely look at me" (Job 30:20, NIV). His words were not neat or polished, yet God did not condemn Job for them. At the end of the book, God rebukes Job's friends, not Job, because they did not speak rightly about Him. Job, however, is not condemned for his honest lament, though God does correct him by revealing His sovereignty (Job 38–41). Job's lament, though messy, was rooted in relationship. He cried out to God rather than walking away from God. And in the end, God lifted his eyes to His majesty and sovereignty: "My ears had heard of you, but now my eyes have seen you" (Job 42:5, NIV). The turn in Job's lament is not the removal of pain, but a clearer vision of God.

The book of Lamentations is filled with the author's laments, in which he pours out his grief over a city in ruins and a people in exile. His prayers are raw: "My eyes fail from weeping, I am in torment within; my heart is poured out on the ground" (Lam. 2:11, NIV). Yet in the middle of the book, he pivots to God's character: "Because of the Lord's great love we are not consumed, for his compassions never fail. They are new every morning; great is your faithfulness" (Lam. 3:22–23, NIV). Lament had not erased his pain, but it had redirected his vision. The anchor in devastation was not an immediate change of circumstance, but God's unchanging compassion and faithfulness.

We learn trust from Jesus. "For the joy set before him he endured the cross" (Heb. 12:2, NIV). He "entrusted himself to him who judges justly" (1 Pet. 2:23, NIV). Trust, for Jesus, meant yielding to the Father's wise and faithful will, not because the path was easy, but because the Father is good. Because Jesus perfectly trusted the Father, we can learn to trust Him in our suffering, too.

This is why lament matters: it is the soil in which trust grows. Honest grief, poured out before God, becomes the doorway to deeper faith. We may not receive a quick resolution. We may not receive the relief we beg for. But we do receive Him, the God whose character does not change. In turning to Him, we also receive hope, because His name reveals His nature and His nature does not shift. He cannot cease to be who He is.

Our God is Healer, whether His healing comes immediately, unfolds over time, or is fulfilled in glory. Our God is Redeemer, so nothing surrendered to Him is beyond restoration. Our God is Peace, bringing His presence to our turmoil and His steadiness to our fear. Our God is Provider, meeting us with enough for today and strength for tomorrow. Our God is Faithful and True; what He promises, He performs, in His wisdom and at His time. He is sovereign and wise; none can thwart His purpose, and His timing is never careless. Our God delights to do the impossible according to His will and purpose, even in the places that seem closed and barren. This is why we can trust Him, not because outcomes are predictable, but because His character is.

Trust grows as we rehearse who God is, not once but daily. We tell our hearts what is true when feelings are loud, and discouragement presses in. We answer our questions with His attributes. When fear says, "You are alone," we remember He is near to all who call on Him in truth. When shame says, "You have failed too deeply," we remember He is gracious and compassionate, slow to anger and abounding in steadfast love. When uncertainty says, "This will never change," we remember that nothing is too hard for the Lord.

Trust also grows as we remember His works. Scripture is a record of God's trustworthy character in action, and our own stories join that record. He sustained Israel in the wilderness. He raised dry bones to life. He brought beauty from ashes (Isaiah 61:3) and joy from mourning. In Christ, all His promises find their "Yes." "He who did not spare his own Son, but gave him up for us all—how will he not also, along with him, graciously give us all things?" (Rom. 8:32, NIV) The cross and the empty tomb are the loudest evidence that He keeps His word.

Because God's character is strong, our trust does not have to be. It can be as small as a mustard seed, yet it clings to a mighty God. Trust is not bravado; it is dependence. It is choosing, in the middle of unanswered questions, to place our weight on who God is. We do not trust because we feel brave; we trust because He is steadfast. We do not trust because we see the outcome; we trust because He is wise and good. We do not trust because life makes sense; we trust because He does not change.

There will be days when trust looks like waiting. Waiting is not a passive void; it is active reliance. We wait by returning to His Word, by recalling His faithfulness, by refusing to draw conclusions about God's character from our pain. We can say, "I do not understand this, but I know You," and that becomes enough light for the next step. The psalmist did not deny his distress; he tethered it to God's steadfast love and faithfulness, and hope rose again.

There will be days when trust looks like obedience without full clarity. Remember Abraham, the man God chose to father a people through whom He would bless the world? In Genesis, God called Abraham to leave his homeland and go to a land He would show him. As Hebrews 11:8 records, Abraham did not receive a map; he received a promise and a call, and he went. We also see this in Mary, a young woman from Nazareth who became the mother of Jesus. When the angel told her she would bear the Son of God, she could not foresee all that her yes would require. Yet she answered, "Let it be to me according to your word" (Luke 1:38, NIV). Obedience, taken one faithful step at a time, becomes a declaration that God's character is a safer foundation than our preferred outcomes.

There will be days when trust looks like receiving manna. God often provides by the day, not by the decade. He gives grace sufficient for today, mercy new this morning, strength for the next act of obedience. As Scripture teaches that His grace is sufficient (2 Corinthians 12:9) and His mercies are new every morning (Lamentations 3:23). He does not promise a stockpile; He promises Himself, and He does not change. That is enough. Daily dependence trains our hearts to love the Giver more than His gifts.

And there will be days when trust looks like surrender. Not resignation, but yieldedness to a Father whose wisdom exceeds ours. Trust does not silence our requests; it anchors them. We still ask boldly, because He invites us to ask. We still knock and seek, because He delights to give good gifts to His children. (Matthew 7:11) Yet beneath and around every petition is a deeper confidence: You are good. You are wise. You will be Yourself toward me. In all of these, trust is simply faith taking the next faithful step.

If we need a simple way to practice this turn, we can answer our doubts with short, steady refrains that fix our eyes on Him. He is faithful, so the future is not fragile. He is good, so His plans are not cruel. He is wise, so His timing is not careless. He is near, so we are not abandoned. He is true, so His promises are not wishful thinking. He is righteous, so His judgments are never unjust. He is sovereign, so nothing can separate us from His love. When trust is hard, remember the times you have witnessed His goodness; yesterday's help is evidence for tomorrow's hope.

Trust does not erase lament; it transforms it. The questions may still rise, the tears may still fall, the body may still hurt, yet beneath it all runs the granite certainty of who God is. He has bound His name to His people and keeps them for His name's sake. He is the same yesterday, today, and forever. He is the Rock that cannot be moved, the Shepherd who carries the weak, the Father who does not leave His children, the Redeemer who restores what is broken. When it is hard to trust, we lean harder into Him.

And in time, we find what believers before us have found. Circumstances may shift, and sometimes they do not, but God remains. His character holds. His Word stands. His presence steadies. Trust grows, not because the path is easy, but because the One who walks with us is faithful and true. Even when trust is hard, God remains trustworthy.

So be bold in your prayers. Pour out your sadness and lament before God, then plant your feet on the solidity of His character and ask Him for what only He can do. Bold prayer does not pretend the pain is small; it brings the whole weight of it to a God who is not small. It names the hurt, asks for wisdom, asks for rescue, asks for daily bread, and keeps asking because His heart is kind and His power is real. Bold prayer is not crossing your fingers or trying to control outcomes; it is leaning on the one true and mighty God who is more than able to answer. We ask big because His mercy is wide. We ask specifically because His attention is personal. We keep knocking because His timing is wise. While you wait, return to Scripture, answer your fears with His promises, and steady your thoughts in what is true about Him. Let your requests be honest and clear: here is what hurts, and here is what I am asking You to do according to Your will and character. Take the next obedient step, then the next, trusting that the One who loves you holds both the long story and today. This is how trust breathes in hard places, and this is how courage rises again: honest lament, specific asks, persevering hope, all resting on the character of God. When it is hard to trust, keep praying boldly. He has not changed. He hears you. He is able.

A Rescue Prayer

Dear God,

Right now, it feels hard to trust You. My circumstances feel unstable, and my heart is torn between what I know of Your goodness and what I see in front of me. Disappointment, hurt, and fear make it difficult to rest in Your promises. I am tempted to rely on myself, to control, to strive, or to shut my heart down so I don't have to hope again. Part of me wants to trust You, and part of me is afraid I will be let down.

But You are not like anyone who has failed me. You are faithful and true. You welcome my questions and do not turn away from my confusion. Your Word shows me that trust is formed in the middle of suffering. You were steadfast with Job and faithful to David in his cries. Your love never ceases, and Your mercies are new every morning. Thank You that Your character is a stronger foundation than my feelings.

So I choose, even with trembling, to trust You again. I lay my fears and disappointments at Your feet. Grow in me a steady trust anchored in who You are. I believe You are faithful, and I will trust You.

In Jesus' name, I pray. Amen.

"Every good and perfect gift is from above, coming down from the Father of the heavenly lights, who does not change like shifting shadows."

James 1:17 (NIV)

CHAPTER

Five

When You Don't Know if God is Good

There are times when the goodness of God seems distant and out of reach. Some days, it feels natural to praise Him; on others, it feels agonizing. There are seasons when we testify with confidence to the kindness of a loving God and seasons when we can only whisper it by faith through tears. When suffering lingers, it becomes a daily companion that wears you down in ways you don't always have words for. In those places, it can feel nearly impossible not just to trust God, but to believe He is still good.

Most of us have heard the saying, "God is good all the time, and all the time, God is good." But what if you know God is good, yet life is so painful that saying it costs you? Sometimes, when we hear "God is good," our hearts respond with a resounding amen, often because we have walked through hard things and seen His kindness up close. Other times, the words land like a weight: "You are telling me God is good, yet deep in my heart I do not feel it." If God is good, why am I suffering like this? Why this sadness and loss? And then there is a quieter response—apathy. We agree in our minds that God is good, yet we do not live like it, walking through our days numb to His presence.

Looking back, the seasons when I struggled most to see God's goodness were, in hindsight, the very seasons when His goodness was powerfully at work in ways I could not yet see. That realization has changed how I hear James's words, "Consider it pure joy, my brothers and sisters, whenever you face trials of many kinds" (James 1:2, NIV). "Consider" is not "feel." It is an act of deliberate accounting, a settled decision to place suffering in a different column because God is doing something real within it. Joy in trial is not denial of pain. It is confidence in purpose.

James tells us why, "because you know that the testing of your faith produces perseverance" (James 1:3, NIV). Trials are not wasted time in God's hands. They grow endurance, the kind that keeps holding when answers do not come quickly. And he adds, "Let perseverance finish its work so that you may be mature and complete, not lacking anything" (James 1:4, NIV). The command to "let" is quiet and courageous. It asks us to stay under what is heavy long enough for God to finish the good work He has begun, trusting that His shaping is not harsh but holy.

James also knows how disorienting suffering can be. Right after he calls us to count it joy, he says, "If any of you lacks wisdom, you should ask God, who gives generously to all without finding fault, and it will be given to you" (James 1:5, NIV). In trial, we need wisdom as much as relief: wisdom to see God's hand, to endure faithfully, to refuse the lie that pain proves God is not good. James later anchors that goodness in God's nature, "Every good and perfect gift is from above, coming down from the Father of the heavenly lights, who does not change like shifting shadows" (James 1:17, NIV). Our circumstances change. He does not.

He is equally clear about another truth we need when we hurt: God is not the author of evil, as Scripture makes clear that He does not tempt anyone (James 1:13). "When tempted, no one should say, 'God is tempting me.' For God cannot be tempted by evil, nor does he tempt anyone" (James 1:13, NIV). Trials come, and they are real, but God meets us within them to refine, not to ruin. For those who endure, James holds out a promise, "Blessed is the one who perseveres under trial because, having stood the test, that person will receive the crown of life that the Lord has promised to those who love him" (James 1:12, NIV). Present endurance is joined to future reward.

So "count it all joy" has come to mean something much simpler and much truer for me: I can be honest about the hurt, I can ask God for wisdom with a secure boldness, and I can still place my suffering in the category of "God is at work here, even if I cannot yet see how." Joy doesn't replace the tears; it sits right beside them. It remembers how God helped me before, looks ahead believing He'll be faithful again, and trusts that even in the hidden and heartbroken places, He is shaping something I wouldn't choose, but may one day thank Him for.

During my dark season, as my physical pain increased and my marriage spiraled toward its end, joy was hard to grasp. Pride stripped away, I came as a daughter asking my heavenly Father for help. Divorce brought danger; my van tires were damaged more than once, my bank account was emptied without my knowledge, the police were called, and threats escalated even after a temporary order of protection was granted. When reunification with their father was ordered, several of my children struggled with suicidal ideations, feeling unheard by the courts. My own physical pain was crushing, but it was nothing compared to watching my children suffer while I fought to keep them safe. It was heartbreaking, and we all felt powerless. Only later, with some distance, could I trace the quiet ways God was already working for our good.

In the middle of what felt uncontrollable, there was one choice left to me: I could run straight into the arms of Jesus and be held in His love, trusting that He was working for my good and His glory. That may sound idealistic given what we were enduring, but deep inside, God supplied the trust and faith I lacked to hold on to that truth.

During that dark time, I sought support from my church. I had raised my children in that church, served on staff, begun and grown ministries there, and I had been richly blessed by the love that so many faithful servants poured out over my family, especially as I struggled to adjust to a life of chronic pain. Church members brought me meals, drove my children to practices, and nourished me with love and encouragement. It was not just a church; it was the Church, as they ministered to me with the hands and feet of Jesus.

However, divorce was more difficult for the church to digest than physical pain. I had grown so used to a marriage that hid what was happening behind closed doors that I believed the right thing was to keep protecting my spouse's reputation, even if it left me isolated and misunderstood. With my whole heart, I hoped that my silence would draw him to church and lead him to surrender to Jesus. In retrospect, I learned that abuse must be brought into the light and that the abuser bears responsibility for any damage to their reputation, since they are the one perpetrating the harm. At the time, though, I was in survival mode, doing the best I knew how to do.

The outcome was that my church mishandled the situation in a deeply painful way. I say this without blame and with much grace, because without being trauma-informed, they lacked the tools and knowledge to support someone walking through what our family was facing. I knew who my husband was and what he was capable of, so while his actions hurt me, they did not shock me. The wound I did not expect came from my church, and it felt like a knife to the chest. Divorce is devastatingly painful, yet what happened with my church remains one of the most hurtful chapters of that season. In the aftermath, the Lord showed me that forgiveness and reconciliation are not the same, that boundaries are actually biblical, and that sometimes the most loving thing you can do is tell the truth, even when it hurts. And even there, God was near, gathering my tears, placing a few steady friends beside me, and preparing a place of healing I could not yet see.

God was working, and although I could only see darkness where I stood, He was already putting things in place for what would become a "count it all joy" moment. On the hardest day of that church hurt, when I had nothing but tears and prayers, my Aunt Carolyn sent me a message. The same aunt who had endured a far greater pain when she lost her only son, Ryan, sent me this promise from Scripture: "Fear not, for I have redeemed you, I have called you by name, you are mine. When you pass through the waters, I will be with you, and through the rivers, they shall not overwhelm you, when you walk through the fire you shall not be burned, and the flame shall not consume you. For I am the Lord your God..." (Isaiah 43:1–3, ESV). I read those words through heartbroken sobs, and they sustained me day after day.

I loved that church deeply, and before that season, I never imagined leaving it. But God, in His wisdom, used that painful experience to move me out of a place where I had grown comfortable and into a place where He could grow me. The pain of what happened in my church became the path into a new church community, as a beloved friend invited me into her church family and walked alongside me while God carried me through the fire. In that church, I found peace, healing, and restoration, and most of all, I experienced the Holy Spirit's power in ways I had never known.

It was not a church of "country club Christians," all coffee, kindness, and smiles while living short of the fullness of God. God placed me in a church where His presence was palpable, so powerful that people were known to burst into tears as soon as they pulled into the parking lot. At every service, God's presence met us. He gently brought hidden things into the light, and He healed the brokenhearted. We left different than we came, not because of hype, but because the Holy Spirit was at work.

Many churches claim to be "praying churches," but that church lived it. Every person was prayed over, and every request was brought before the Lord. The most important service of the week was not Sunday; it was the Wednesday night prayer meeting. In a room of thousands, we were each given prayer cards with other members' requests, collected in advance so that every need was covered. We prayed in unity for one another, and more than once, the card in my hand, written by someone I had never met, echoed the very needs in my own heart. It felt like a whisper from God, "I see you, I hear you, and I am working for your good. Your needs are not forgotten. Someone is praying for you now, even as you pray for them with a heart that sees their pain."

At the prayer service, we poured out prayers for others, we were nourished with strong biblical teaching, and we flooded the altars asking for more of whatever God had for us. Apathy may have walked in with us, but at the altar, expectation took its place, a bold confidence that God meets His people as they seek Him.

There, my hope was renewed. God brought to mind the many ways He had helped me before: timely Scripture that strengthened me, the practical care that showed up when I had nothing left, the quiet provisions that covered needs I hadn't even voiced, and the peace that settled over me when fear fought to defeat me. Remembering God's help didn't erase the pain, but it reoriented my heart and taught me to pray boldly again; the God who helped me then would be faithful to me now.

Bold prayer is not bold for the sake of being demanding; it is honest, steady, and expectant. When God's goodness feels far, you can still come. You can count what you cannot yet feel, you can ask Him for wisdom, and you can stay under His shaping with trust. Bring Him your amen and your agony. Name your apathy and set it down. Remember His past faithfulness. He has not changed. His presence still meets His people, and His Word still holds in the fire and the flood.

So pray the kind of prayers that carry both tears and confidence. Pray for others as if their card were in your hands. Pray for yourself as one who is seen and heard. Keep coming before Him with a heart that expects Him to work. Joy may sit beside your sorrow for a while, but it will not be empty. The same God who helped you before will help you now. And as you keep praying boldly, bringing Him both your questions and your trust, you will find, in time, that He has been near all along, even when His goodness felt far away.

A Rescue Prayer

Dear God,

There are moments when it's hard to believe that You are good. My life has held so much pain and disappointment that those words can feel hollow. I hear others say it, yet part of me wonders how it can be true when my story feels so bruised. I don't want to pretend or force praise. I want to believe You are good, but sometimes my heart struggles to agree.

But Your Word says that every good and perfect gift comes from You and that You do not change. You are not the author of harm. You meet Your people in the fire and in the flood, and You promise they will not be overcome. You are the Father who runs toward the prodigal, the Shepherd who seeks the lost, and the Savior who gave His life for me. Thank You that Your goodness does not depend on my understanding.

So I ask for faith to see Your goodness again. Open my eyes to Your kindness, even here. Heal the places where hurt has shaped how I see You. Help me bring my questions to You and not turn away. I trust that You are good, You are present, and You are still at work.

In Jesus' name, I pray. Amen.

"Thus far the Lord has helped us."

1 Samuel 7:12 (NIV)

CHAPTER

Six

When Confidence Is Shaken

There are times when we cannot trace God's hand, yet we cling to trust in His heart. In quiet devastation, when answers seem delayed, and the way ahead is unclear, faith holds to what we know of Him, not what we feel in the moment. God sees, He hears, He is near, and He is at work according to His purposes for our good and His glory, even when we cannot see how.

One way we learn confidence in God is by remembering. In Scripture, we see this kind of remembrance in what Samuel called an Ebenezer, stones of help that mark where God met us and carried us. As we begin to name them, simple and specific, our hearts learn to say, "Thus far the Lord has helped me" (1 Samuel 7:12, NIV), and to pray with a calm expectation that He will help again. You may already carry a few of these stones in your own story, small but weighty, enough to hold your footing today.

In the midst of turmoil, God rebuilt my trust one Ebenezer at a time. Before I could see answers to my desperate prayers, He turned my eyes to the times He had already made the impossible possible. Memory can do that for a pain-filled heart; it reminds us of yesterday's help to silence the discouragement of today.

For the last several years of my marriage, aside from ministry, I was a stay-at-home mom. Managing a busy family while battling chronic pain made outside work unrealistic, and our household relied on my husband's income. He tightly controlled our finances, and when I filed for divorce, he cut off support to the children and to me. A few weeks later, on my birthday, as my kids snuggled up to watch a movie and order pizza, I discovered he had closed my personal bank account, the one I had held since college. The timing felt deliberate, meant to inflict pain, and I was left with no income, no account, and no idea how I would make it. I sobbed myself sick and poured out my heart to God, begging Him for help.

I wish I could say that my prayer in that moment opened the floodgates of heaven, and we were overwhelmed with provision. That was not what occurred, but God was still working beneath the surface, and He reminded me of one of my very first Ebenezers. Delays do not mean the absence of God, and quiet does not mean indifference; often, the first mercy is the one that helps us remember.

As a little girl, I could not stop moving. I cartwheeled, climbed, and tumbled. I jumped, I fidgeted, I raced. I was all action and go, and I still am, just with better self-control now. Inspired by Mary Lou Retton winning gold at the 1984 Olympics, my mom determined that gymnastics was a natural fit for me. The coaches seemed to agree, and I was quickly moved into a team program at a local gymnastics gym. I loved gymnastics. I lived and breathed it. When I was at the gym, my heart was happy, and when I was at home, I was practicing to be back in the gym.

The better I became at gymnastics, the larger the financial burden grew to pay for practices, coaching, and competitions. Paired with the increasing time commitments, my parents decided they could no longer afford for me to continue. To say I was devastated is an understatement. As a member of a growing family that would eventually include nine children, I always knew finances were tight. It was a struggle to feed and house us all on my dad's minister's salary, so I understood when an extra cost like gymnastics had to be eliminated. Understanding, however, did not make me long for it any less. I still tumbled everywhere I went. Beds became trampolines, curbs became balance beams, and my younger siblings became recruits in my home-coaching endeavors as we flipped off an old rebounder trampoline onto a torn mattress and makeshift mats.

Every day I prayed that God would make a way for me to do gymnastics again. Two years passed, and that prayer seemed unanswered, yet I still hoped. Each year, our school held a talent show, and it was my tradition to perform a simple floor routine, nothing incredible or polished. I choreographed my own moves to music I had recorded on a cassette from a record player, then tumbled back and forth across the stage.

That year, a mom in the audience asked my mom if I was still in gymnastics. My mom answered honestly, "No," and explained why. The Holy Spirit used that small conversation to stir that precious woman's heart, and she offered to pay for an entire year of my gymnastics. God answered my prayer.

To my memory, this was my first significant Ebenezer. God answered the desires of my heart, desires He had prompted me to pray about. He answered my persistent prayer, and through it I learned that He cared deeply about me, even in something as seemingly insignificant as the sport I loved. When I was placed back on the gymnastics team, I was so weak from being out of the sport for several years that I struggled to keep up, but I outworked everyone. Quiet and shy, while others were talking, I was working. My return to gymnastics was hard-won, and I was not going to waste it. When the year of financing ended, my parents went to withdraw me, but because of my positive attitude and strong work ethic, my coach advocated with the gym on my behalf. In another answer to prayer, the gym allowed me to help coach other classes in exchange for my tuition. This Ebenezer became one of the anchors of my faith life. My requests mattered to God. I have returned to this memory many times when my confidence was shaken. First stones matter; they teach us how to stand and how to recognize the next one God places on the path.

I did not know it then, but God would use that provision to open doors in my future. It did not make me an Olympic gymnast, but it let me regain lost skills, gain new ones, and carry hard-earned discipline forward. That Ebenezer became a bridge from gymnastics into cheerleading and, in time, to a college scholarship at Morehead State University, a Division I school with the best coed cheerleading program in the nation. Along the way, I earned three national championships and, more importantly, I was formed by coaches, mentors, and teammates who loved me, refined me, and called out the best in me.

Cheerleading also set the stage for the beginning of my family. I married during college, and I welcomed my first baby while I was still cheering, and my team, coaches, and university family surrounded us with practical help and steady encouragement. At my university, God strengthened my public speaking through formal training and real opportunities, shaping a gift He would later use to preach and teach His Word. The discipline I learned on the mat carried into every part of life, teaching me to show up, to prepare, to practice until excellence became muscle memory, to keep going when it hurt, and to finish with integrity. Those habits have served me as a mother, in ministry, and at work. Looking back, I can see how that first answered prayer became a stone I would stand on again and again, a memory that reminded me to ask boldly and trust God to work.

That first Ebenezer was one of many I would stand on when the ground seemed to shift beneath my feet. As I wrestled with the uncertainty of leaving a destructive marriage, looking to my Ebenezers helped me place certainty in God's character rather than my circumstances, in His proven faithfulness rather than my frail feelings, in who He is rather than how today looked. Remembering steadied my steps and rekindled expectancy when fear tried to speak lies over my life. Courage often returns this way, not in a surge, but in a surety, as remembrance makes room for expectation. So I began to name my Ebenezers, simple and specific, remembering the times He provided, the moments He protected, the guidance He gave, the strength He supplied.

In that seemingly endless season of difficulty, when I looked at my Ebenezers, I could undoubtedly see that God had always been working for my good, and it strengthened my faith that my children and I would be safe again.

With no money coming in, the court ordered a temporary amount to care for the children and me, an amount that would not make ends meet. When I stared at what I lacked, I could not see how we would make it another day, but when I looked at my Ebenezers, I knew God was my Provider. Even then, He supplied through unexpected sources: weekend meals tucked into backpacks by a caring school, winter coats and warm clothes from a nearby clothing bank, food staples from the pantry at our new church. Friends opened their homes and holidays to us, and family sent what they could. It was an agonizing season of uncertainty and court appearances, but God was not distant for a moment. He was undeniably present. Every tear I cried, He was there. Every prayer I prayed, He met me with reassurance and strength. He was teaching me to trust Him with a bold faith when I could not see a way forward beyond surviving the next moment.

Ironically, in that season of endless bills and lawyer fees piling far higher than I could pay, the Lord pressed on my heart to tithe anyway, to give the firstfruits of everything He placed in my hands back to Him (Proverbs 3:9–10, NIV). It felt impossible to give when I did not have enough to begin with, so I started giving through tears, a costly obedience. That obedience ended up being a mercy. It reminded me that everything I have is the Lord's and I'm just stewarding it. When I opened my hands, I learned to trust God with what was already His anyway. This gave me the gift of seeing how God provides daily, just as He did for the Israelites with manna in the wilderness, giving exactly what was needed for each day (Exodus 16).

God did not erase every bill overnight, but He met us again and again. Needs were covered in ways I could not have orchestrated, and provisions arrived at the right time. The math still looked impossible on paper, yet we lacked no true necessity. At the same time, He gave me wisdom to live within new limits, to budget carefully, to say no without shame, to sell what we did not need, and to receive help without apology. We prayed over the little we set aside each week, and my children watched God answer in small, powerful ways. Tithing did not turn into instant abundance, but it did reorient my heart. Each provision became another Ebenezer, a simple stone that said, "He will be faithful here too."

As I surrendered my finances and future to God, He pressed even closer to what I treasured most: my children. In prayer, I sensed His gentle question, "Do you trust Me with them, too? I love them more than you can imagine." That convicted me to the core. He was not asking me to stop fighting for their safety or to step back from wise action. He was asking me to release the fear that tried to control every outcome while trusting Him with everything. Surrender is not stepping back from love; it is stepping deeper into it, trusting the Father wholeheartedly while you keep walking in His will.

Fearful, I turned to my Ebenezers to remember His faithfulness, and there I saw two memories of moments when my prayerful trust for my children was met with beautiful, abundant healing. The first came before my second daughter was two, when she had three unexplained grand mal, or tonic-clonic, seizures. After several days in the hospital, she was diagnosed with epilepsy, and we were sent home with sobering warnings about what her future could hold. Her epilepsy diagnosis terrified me because a close relative had been tormented by epilepsy throughout their life. I prayed over my daughter constantly, asking God to heal her, and each year she remained seizure-free, I rejoiced. Eventually, she was declared completely free of epilepsy, a miracle birthed through the power of prayer and the kindness of a loving God.

Another healing that echoed in my heart as I learned to entrust my children to God was that of my youngest son. As an infant, he was diagnosed with severe torticollis, his head dramatically tilted to one side, so much so that his sweet little face began to flatten on the side that rested against his left shoulder. His physical therapist called it "the worst case of torticollis she had ever seen." For months, I worked with her, stretching and strengthening my baby in hopes of recovery, but he was not improving. Finally, she said, "At this point, there are only two options: a course of Botox treatments or surgery." Both possibilities frightened me, so I asked a group of mom friends to pray.

After they spent time interceding, I began to see dramatic improvement in my son's torticollis. It was as if his neck had straightened overnight. When I took him back to the therapist, she was astounded. "This is truly a miracle," she said. Her measurements agreed; visit after visit, she had charted the tilt of his neck with virtually no change, until that day. He was healed. All glory to God. His healing is evident to this day; even the facial flattening disappeared, and he is a healthy young man with no visible sign that he ever had severe torticollis.

I clung to these two Ebenezers as several of my children struggled with severe depression in those years of hardship and instability. I prayed fervently for them, and I asked God to heal the chronic pain that plagued me. The same God who had healed my children before could heal and protect them now, and He could do the same for me. Breakthrough was coming.

Remembering my Ebenezers did not remove the hardship; it kept me focused on the heart of my Heavenly Father. Each stone of remembrance testified that the God who had worked miraculously before was still working in my present circumstances. The God who provided when I was a child, who carried me as a young mother, who met us in courtrooms and waiting rooms and at crowded altars, is the same God who hears me now, and He hears you too. So keep praying, just as Jesus taught us to pray and not give up (Luke 18:1, NIV). Pray in the darkness, pray in the loneliness, pray in the heartache, pray in the pain; pray continually (1 Thessalonians 5:17, NIV). Pray when you do not see a path, trusting that He is working and that He will make a way.

Bold prayer does not deny the agony of pain; it persists, choosing to remain confident in the power of a present and unchanging God. He does not change. The God who rescued you before will rescue you again. And if you cannot see His hand, or doubt that you ever have, cry out and ask Him to show you where He has helped you. He loves you, and He has been working for your good. Look to your Ebenezers for confidence to keep praying and to believe that He will work. You do not have to feel brave to pray boldly; you only have to come as you are to the God who sees, who hears, and who acts.

A Rescue Prayer

Dear God,

My confidence has been shaken. What once felt stable now feels uncertain, and I am unsteady. Fear and what-ifs crowd my thoughts, and I struggle to believe that You will come through for me. It is hard to pray boldly when I don't feel secure.

But You are the God who has helped me again and again. Your Word and my own story remind me of Your faithfulness. You provide in the wilderness, heal what is broken, and sustain Your people. You have been faithful across generations, and You have been faithful to me. Thank You that my confidence does not rest in my strength, but in Your unchanging character.

So I choose to remember. Bring to mind the moments when You made a way, answered a prayer, or carried me when I could not stand. Let those memories strengthen my heart to trust You again. When doubt rises, remind me of how You have helped me thus far. Build in me a steady confidence that expects You to move. I believe that the God who was faithful before is still at work in my life today.

In Jesus' name, I pray. Amen.

"My grace is sufficient for you, for my power is made perfect in weakness."

2 Corinthians 12:9 (NIV)

CHAPTER

Seven

When You Have Nothing Left

Have you ever felt completely emptied out, too hurt, too broken, too heavy with sorrow to offer anything to anyone, even to God? That was me. I wanted strength, but all I had was weakness. "My grace is sufficient for you, for my power is made perfect in weakness" (2 Corinthians 12:9, NIV).

There's strength in surrender. I know that sounds counterintuitive, but there is so much strength in giving everything over to God, getting out of His way, and watching Him work. When we do this, we stop being a barrier to the work He's doing in us and begin to receive blessings as we partner with Him and allow His will to be done. Easier said than done, right? Yet that place of surrender became the very place where I found my strength in the Lord.

At my praying church, even through very difficult circumstances, God kept nurturing me. I was being fed powerful truths from Scripture every Sunday, and on Wednesday nights, the prayer service ministered to my spirit in ways I can hardly describe. My quiet times in the Word were bolstered by that encouragement, yet my journals from that season are full of daily, desperate pleas for God to move mightily in my circumstances. The physical pain I was barely managing was made worse by the stress of the divorce and the constant fear for my children. The pain and fatigue compounded the emotional strain, but I had no choice except to keep treading water, trying to stay afloat when I felt like I was drowning.

Our church regularly opened the altars for people to bring their requests to the Lord. I didn't come from a background where altar time was typical, so at first I stayed glued to my seat, dismissing it as unnecessary and too emotional. Patient with me, God kept nudging my heart to walk forward for prayer. The first time I did, He met me there. Yes, God often met me in my seat, but He had something uniquely special for me whenever I put "feet to my faith" and went forward to pray or be prayed for. That act of surrender became a constant for me: a beautiful exchange where I gave Him my fear, petitions, worry, control, and weakness, and received His grace, mercy, help, and unmerited favor.

One Wednesday night, I arrived early, like always, to sit near the front. When the doors opened, people poured in, hungry to see how the Lord would move. I found my seat and saved one for a friend. I desperately wanted to be there, surrounded by prayer, but the heaviness in my heart hurt so much that it had almost been too much to attend.

Everything felt like it was going wrong. My children were suffering, my health was in shambles, my heart was distraught, and my future was beyond uncertain. My only hope was what the Lord could do. That night, the minister spoke briefly about Pentecost and the outpouring of the Holy Spirit in Acts. I knew I needed that. I needed more of whatever God had for me: empowerment through His Spirit and a fresh outpouring every single day.

The minister then explained that the rest of the service would simply be time to pray, to ask God for more, and watch Him move. I rushed to the altar, pacing back and forth as I petitioned the Lord for more. I had nothing to give Him, but I gave everything over to Him. In that moment of surrender, I was met with His strength. The Holy Spirit poured out over me so powerfully that I found myself on my knees, arms raised, tears streaming down my face, His words spilling from my mouth. It was the holy presence and power of God's Spirit. "Peace I leave with you, my peace I give you" (John 14:27, NIV). I felt a love, a peace, and a comfort unlike anything I had ever known.

That moment moved my life in a different direction. I had long been a believer, but something shifted deep inside me. I was given a certainty that didn't come from me. In surrender, God empowered me by His Holy Spirit. Instead of living by what I could see or manage, I began to notice the Spirit at work in ways only God could do. In the outpouring, there was deliverance. Intrusive thoughts were silenced. Peace settled where fear had ruled. Confusion became clarity. My attention became laser-focused on growing in the Lord. Casual commitment gave way to a Spirit-led zeal. The legal battle remained, my body still hurt, my future was still uncertain, but the Holy Spirit was doing something bigger than all those things.

Here's what I needed then and what I still need now: not a little encouragement, but an outpouring. I don't just need to try harder; I need the Helper. The Spirit doesn't simply soothe; He strengthens me to stand. He doesn't only comfort; He leads and sends me. "You will receive power when the Holy Spirit comes on you, and you will be my witnesses...to the ends of the earth" (Acts 1:8, NIV).

Surrender didn't make me passive; it made me available. It didn't mean doing nothing; it meant allowing Him to work without me getting in the way. Practically, it meant walking in His will, praying first, obeying quickly, and trusting God with the parts I couldn't fix. Day by day, He strengthened me to show up for my kids, to tell the truth without fear, to steward what little I had, and to keep coming back to the altar, at church and at home.

Here is what I learned in that season and keep relearning now: boldness doesn't always feel like fire. Sometimes it feels like breath. It is the steady inhale of trust and the exhale of surrender. It is praying big when your voice shakes. It is standing on what God has already done and asking Him to do it again. It is believing that the same Spirit who raised Jesus from the dead is working in the dark edges of your story, even when you cannot see any light at all. And when He pours out, He doesn't stop at "enough"; He draws you into more than you imagined.

That outpouring wasn't just for a moment; it became a daily renewal. Every time I felt depleted, I asked the Lord to give me more, a fresh outpouring of His Spirit for that day, and He did. Even in that season of great hardship, I realized the greatest gift I could give my children was to prioritize growing in the Lord so the healing effects of my surrender would flow over them like a balm. As I drew closer to the Lord, my witness multiplied. I couldn't stop talking about Jesus. He was meeting me every single day in unexpected ways and in moves of great power.

As the Lord kept meeting me in prayer, my heart kept returning to a passage in the Bible about the early church. I thought about how the Spirit's outpouring did not end at Pentecost; it kept propelling them into more. In Acts 3, Peter and John met a man who had been lame from birth. Peter spoke healing in Jesus' name, and the man stood and walked. That public healing created a holy disturbance. Crowds gathered, the gospel was preached, and almost immediately, opposition followed. By Acts 4, Peter and John were arrested, questioned, and commanded to be silent about Jesus. The clash between Spirit-birthed boldness and surrounding threats was unavoidable.

The miracle was awe-inspiring, but the church's response when pressure mounted is what ministers to my heart. The apostles were warned to stop speaking in the name of Jesus, yet they answered with bold purpose and clarity, "We cannot help speaking about what we have seen and heard" (Acts 4:20, NIV).

That sentence lives in me. The Spirit does not manufacture bravado; He produces witness. When He fills us, we begin speaking about what we have truly seen and heard of Jesus. We do not wait for the hard times to disappear; we bear witness to what God is doing in those times, because He is always working.

Released to their own people, Peter and John returned to the church, and instead of retreating, they prayed. They did not draft a strategy first, and they did not bargain for safety. Together they lifted their voices, "Sovereign Lord," anchoring themselves in who God is before asking Him for anything. They remembered Scripture, they named the opposition, and then they asked for more, not less. "Now, Lord, consider their threats and enable your servants to speak your word with great boldness. Stretch out your hand to heal and perform signs and wonders through the name of your holy servant Jesus" (Acts 4:29–30, NIV). That is what I wanted, and what I still want now: less fear, less worry, and more boldness that comes from His presence and power.

God answered them. "After they prayed, the place where they were meeting was shaken. And they were all filled with the Holy Spirit and spoke the word of God boldly" (Acts 4:31, NIV). Not just the apostles, all of them. Not a one-time courage, but a fresh filling that turned pressure into proclamation, threat into testimony, need into dependence, and dependence into power. This is the pattern I keep praying for in my own life: anchored in who God is, honest about what I face, and asking for more of His Spirit so I keep speaking, loving, praying, and moving forward with holy boldness.

This example continued to challenge my prayers. Instead of rushing my requests to the front, I lifted my eyes first. I named who God is, I remembered what He has said, I set the truth of my circumstance before Him, and then I asked for courage and for His hand to move. When the early church prayed that way, the room did not applaud their resolve; the room shook with God's presence. The shaking did not promise ease. It brought a strength that held them steady, endurance to keep going, unity when pressure could have divided them, generosity that met real needs, and a witness that refused to quit.

That was what I needed, not ease (although that would have been nice), but endurance; not my plan, but God's presence. Their story spoke hope to my own. When pressure closed in, and my strength was gone, my prayer grew simple and steady: "Sovereign Lord, You see. You hear. You are near. Consider these threats against my peace and my family, and enable me to speak Your word with boldness. Stretch out Your hand to heal what is broken in our bodies and in our home." If God shook that house in Jerusalem, He could shake the atmosphere of my heart and give me courage to declare His victory before I could see it.

The fruit of that prayer spilled into ordinary days. Luke writes that all the believers were one in heart and mind; great grace was upon them all. Needs were met, resources were shared, and the church became a living answer to its own prayer. I saw echoes of that in our story, too. As the Spirit kept filling and refilling, kindness rose up around us, generosity found us, and faith held us. When I needed help and seemingly had no one, the Lord put the right people beside us at just the right times. That ancient pattern of Acts kept unfolding in modern clothes.

Acts 4 also gave me language for holy defiance, not rebellion against people, but allegiance to Jesus when fear tries to govern our choices. When the council ordered silence, Peter and John answered, "Which is right in God's eyes, to listen to you, or to him?" (Acts 4:19, NIV). In the cries of our own crisis, that question clarified so much. "Which is right in God's eyes today: to listen to fear or to Him, to listen to shame or to Him, to listen to exhaustion that says quit or to Him." My boldness became pleasing no one but God, and trusting Him with the outcome.

My desperate prayers were reshaped from "Lord, make this easier" to "Lord, make me faithful. Fill me with a fresh outpouring of Your Spirit every day, and help me to fulfill Your will for my life." I asked for signs and wonders because Scripture teaches me to, and I asked for daily bread because Jesus taught me to. I asked for the miraculous because not only did I desperately need miracles, but we serve a God who delights in doing the miraculous in accordance with His will. I asked for healings that only God could do and for the capacity to keep putting one foot in front of the other when everything felt overwhelmingly difficult. The Spirit answered in both registers, sometimes in power that took my breath, and other times in peace that held me as I cried in secret.

The pattern holds for you too: stay close to Jesus, pray, receive His power, and keep seeking His will. Be with Jesus. Open Scripture and let it minister to you. Come to the altar, whether it be at church or at your kitchen table, and pray the kind of prayers that begin with His character and end with His mission. Ask for boldness to speak and live the gospel. Ask for His hand to heal minds and bodies, for signs and wonders that point to Jesus, not to us. Ask for the place you stand to shake with His presence, then get up and love the people in front of you.

If you are walking into a meeting that scares you, the Acts 4 prayer belongs on your lips. If you are parenting through a storm, it belongs in your household. If you are waiting for test results, prayer belongs in your car in the hospital parking lot. If you are carrying grief or chronic pain, it belongs in the middle of your night. "Now, Lord, consider their threats and enable your servants to speak your word with great boldness." He still answers that prayer. He still fills. He still heals. He still restores. He still makes ordinary people into witnesses.

Sometimes the hardest part of prayer is simply knowing where to begin, especially when you're tired, worn down, or unsure of what you even need. So here's how I'm practicing it now, and how you can practice it too: start by lifting your eyes before you lift your requests. Begin by saying who God is: Sovereign Lord, Father, faithful and near. Remember His Word, the promises that stand steady when your emotions feel unstable. Lay the truth of your situation at His feet without minimizing it or pretending it's smaller than it is. Then ask Him for more of His Spirit: more boldness to pray and speak and act in love, more healing where things are broken, more freedom where something has held you captive, more wisdom where you feel confused, more unity in your home and church, more generosity that meets real needs. And then look for even a small way to obey. Bold prayer and faithful action always travel together.

When Peter and John walked back out of that prayer meeting, their world had not changed, but they had. That is the gift of the Spirit. The threats did not evaporate, but fear lost its voice. The pressures did not disappear, but grace grew larger than anxiety. The mission did not shrink; it sharpened. They spoke the word of God boldly, and they kept at it.

That is where I want to live, not at the mercy of my limits, but carried by the Spirit who loves to fill empty places. Not silenced by opposition, but strengthened to speak life. Not isolated by pain, but knit into a people who pray until the ground shakes and needs are met. Not waiting for ideal conditions, but moving with Jesus in the real world, one surrendered and wholly submitted yes at a time.

If boldness today feels more like breath than fire, that is all right. Breathe in trust, breathe out surrender. Be with Jesus. Pray the church's prayer. Ask for His hand to move. Be faithful to obey and ask for all He has for you. And when He pours out, do not stop at "enough"; let Him propel you into more.

A Rescue Prayer

Dear God,

I feel empty and worn out. I have tried to be strong for so long that I have nothing left to give. My emotions, my body, and my mind are tired. I am overwhelmed by what I cannot fix and exhausted by what I cannot carry. I know I should come to You, but even prayer feels heavy when I feel this depleted.

But Your Word says that Your power is made perfect in weakness. When I am weak, You are strong in me. You give strength to the weary and fill what is empty. You poured out Your Spirit on ordinary people and made them bold. You still fill empty vessels. Thank You that I don't have to bring You strength—only surrender.

So I come to You with what feels like nothing and place it in Your hands. Fill me with Your Holy Spirit. Renew what is dry and restore what is weary. Replace my exhaustion with Your peace and strength. Teach me to live from surrender, not striving. Let my weakness become the place where Your presence is most evident. I trust You to fill what I cannot.

In Jesus' name, I pray. Amen.

"See, I am doing a new thing! Now it springs up; do you not perceive it? I am making a way in the wilderness and streams in the wasteland."

Isaiah 43:19 (NIV)

CHAPTER

Eight

When You Need Breakthrough

Sometimes the ground will not give. You pray, you plead, you repent, you obey when it is difficult, and still it seems as if you are stuck in a mire of suffering and difficult circumstances that refuse to change. That was the season when I stopped asking only for what my limited faith could envision and began asking God for breakthrough. I implored Him to do what I could not, to move mountains that seemed immovable and overcome what looked impossible.

In those months, the worship song *"Do It Again"* became my prayer in a melody. Two lines looped in my spirit: *"I've seen You move,"* and *"I'll see You do it again."* I was not borrowing hype; I was rehearsing history. God had already moved mountains in my story, and worship helped me anchor to His track record while I waited on His timetable. When my own words ran out, the song handed me a simple confession of faith: "You have made a way before, and I believe You will make a way again." I did not know it then, but years later, my mom would tell me she had been clinging to the same truths from Scripture found in that song as she fought for me in prayer.

Scripture names God as the One who breaks through. David called the battlefield *Baal-Perazim*, "the Lord who breaks out," because God surged like rushing waters and the tide turned (2 Samuel 5:20, NIV). The prophets echo the same promise: God goes before His people, levels what stands high, and makes a way in places that look like wasteland (Isaiah 45:2; 43:19, NIV). These are not slogans; they are reminders of who He is. So I prayed with expectation, not because I could engineer an outcome, but because His character has not changed.

For me, breakthrough did not arrive as a sudden deluge. It began with daily submission. I started asking God to do the impossible. I set aside my own will, prayed for His, and brought Him every place where a barricade stood. I stopped limiting my prayers to what looked achievable and began asking Him for breakthrough in places where victory felt out of reach.

Determined to persist until mountains moved, I began with fasting. In Scripture, fasting is not a means of earning answers. It is a way of seeking God with a whole heart. He invites His people to return to Him with fasting, weeping, and mourning (Joel 2:12, NIV). Isaiah describes fasting as alignment with God's will, the kind that loosens chains, lifts oppression, and breaks every yoke (Isaiah 58:6, NIV). Across Scripture we see the same pattern: Esther fasted and God opened a door no one could shut (Esther 4:16, NIV); Jehoshaphat proclaimed a fast and the Lord fought for Judah (2 Chronicles 20:3–22, NIV); Ezra fasted for protection and God answered (Ezra 8:21–23, NIV); Daniel fasted and wisdom came (Daniel 9:3; 10:2–3, NIV). Jesus said, "when you fast," not "if you fast" (Matthew 6:16–18, NIV). He Himself fasted before His ministry began (Matthew 4:1–2, NIV), and the early church fasted as they sought God's direction (Acts 13:2–3; 14:23, NIV). Fasting does not manipulate God; it makes room for Him. It quiets noise, sharpens discernment, humbles the heart, and unites prayer so we can recognize His hand when it moves.

I prayed about the fast God wanted me to undertake and sensed Him directing me to a twenty-one-day Daniel Fast. Aside from the safety and protection of my children, my most urgent need was my health. I had started weaning off prescriptions, but the change catapulted me into excruciating pain. I saw no path forward without God's intervention. So I prayed for a breakthrough.

In addition to nerve pain, I battled chronic fatigue, fibromyalgia, and frequent migraines. Even my "good" pain days were miserable. I begged God for relief and persisted in prayer.

I was also being crushed financially. Every pay period, I tithed through tears. I had not yet become a joyful giver, and every month I ended with negative funds in my account. The legal battles were multiplying expenses and our twelve-passenger van needed major, unexpected repairs. I could not see any path to financial safety. So I continued to pray for breakthrough.

I needed a job to provide for my children, but I did not see how I could work with my health needs and our family schedule. I applied for positions and prayed for God to move in power.

These were only a few of the needs I kept bringing before the Lord. I held tightly to this promise contained in scripture: God is able to do immeasurably more than all we ask or imagine (Ephesians 3:20–21, NIV).

The first breakthrough came even before the fast began. My health insurance had disappeared, and a major shift in my pain came unexpectedly through illness. A severe case of gastroenteritis left me unable to keep anything down, including the medications I had been trying to taper. It was miserable, violent sickness that brought shaking, crying, dehydration, and total body weakness. I was so weak my legs would not hold me, and I could barely crawl. I knew I should go to the hospital, but I could not afford another bill. When I finally recovered enough to stand, I made the decision not to return to those medications. I still had pain, but God sustained me as I stayed off them and endured.

After years of praying, surrender and fasting marked the turning point. Barriers that had felt locked in stone began to give way. During the fast, my fibromyalgia eased, migraines calmed, and years of chronic fatigue lifted. By day twenty-one, the change was unmistakable, so I extended the fast to thirty days. In the months that followed, it became clear that God had brought significant healing in my body. My migraines became rare, fibromyalgia flare-ups were infrequent, and the chronic fatigue that had defined my life simply vanished. It felt like emerging from a dark cave into sunlight.

Financially, I still struggle at times, but I now tithe with joy because I have seen God multiply what I give back to Him. One answer began with a rejection. I applied for a job I was more than qualified for, but the night before I heard back, I prayed a simple line in my journal: "Dear Lord, please provide continued opportunities for me to make money." It was honest and aligned with Scripture: all hard work brings profit (Proverbs 14:23, NIV).

The next day, I learned I did not get the position. That same afternoon, a lifelong publishing executive from the church I grew up in, someone I had not spoken to in twenty years, messaged me and offered $200 to review writing for a client, with the possibility of ghostwriting a book afterward. In a season when I was sacrificing meals so my children could eat, that $200 felt like manna. It touched a deep desire I had written in my journal not long before: my dream job would be in publishing. I had done nothing to make it happen except pray, yet God placed that message in my inbox at the exact moment I needed it.

That small job became a doorway. It eventually led to a fulfilling publishing career, from ghostwriting books to serving as the company's vice president, to helping create *Rescue Prayers*.

Those breakthroughs paved the way for something even greater, something that once felt impossible.

When I think about breakthrough, my heart goes to biblical Hannah. She faced an immovable mountain: infertility. She wept, fasted, prayed, and returned to the temple year after year. Misunderstood by those around her, she poured out her soul before the Lord (1 Samuel 1:10, NIV). She prayed specifically and submitted completely. She asked for a son and promised to dedicate him to God. Her vow was trust, not bargaining. Even when Eli misunderstood her silent prayer, she stayed fixed on God.

Then two things happened. Her prayer produced inner release; she entrusted the burden to God, and Eli blessed her request. Scripture says she went away, ate, and her face was no longer downcast (1 Samuel 1:18, NIV). The circumstance had not changed, but her posture had. She poured out her soul and walked in peace.

Then comes the line that steadies me: "The Lord remembered her" (1 Samuel 1:19, NIV). Not that God had forgotten, but that He acted in His time. Hannah conceived and bore Samuel, and true to her vow, she returned him to God.

Hannah's pattern matters for us: come honestly, ask specifically, surrender completely, receive blessing gratefully, return what God gives with obedience, and walk in peace while you wait.

When a breakthrough is needed, you can borrow the shape of her bold prayer: "Lord, You know this need. If You grant it, I will use it for Your glory. My family, my future, my work, my health; they are Yours. Break through in Your way and Your time, and make my life a testimony that says, 'It is not by strength that one prevails.'"

A Rescue Prayer

Dear God,

I feel stuck and worn down. I have prayed and waited, yet some things still feel immovable. There are needs I cannot meet, battles I cannot win, and situations I cannot change. My heart is tired of facing the same walls. I need You to do what I cannot. I need breakthrough.

But You are the God who breaks through. You go before Your people, level what is too high, and make a way in the wilderness. You remembered Hannah in her distress and turned her sorrow into praise. Nothing is too hard for You. Thank You that seeking You is never in vain, because You are a living and powerful God who still moves.

So I come to You boldly, asking for breakthrough in every place I feel stuck. Show me how to seek You with my whole heart and surrender to Your will. I place my life in Your hands. Move in Your way and in Your time. Let my life be a testimony that it was not by my strength, but by Yours. I trust that You are already at work.

In Jesus' name, I pray. Amen.

"For we live by faith, not by sight."

2 Corinthians 5:7 (NIV)

CHAPTER

Nine

When You Need to Prepare for a Promise

Sometimes God speaks a word to your heart, even when all you can see around you says, "Not yet." The timeline is unclear, the pathway is hidden, and still the Spirit quietly asks you to hold what He has spoken and get ready. This is faith, not wishful thinking, but preparing steadily for what God has spoken, trusting Him with how and when it unfolds. "Blessed is she who has believed that the Lord would fulfill his promises to her" (Luke 1:45, NIV). When we believe God has spoken a promise to our hearts, we don't ignore or squander it; we pray bold prayers and take the first obedient steps, trusting that what we cannot yet see, God is already shaping. "For we live by faith, not by sight" (2 Corinthians 5:7, NIV).

This call to prepare for a promise you can't yet see has been a recurring theme in my life. Long before I became a professional writer, God gave me a simple word: "Write." That word held a promise, one that, when practiced in obedience, would one day produce a bountiful harvest as writing became my vocation. At the time, I had no idea where it would lead. I only knew I had to walk in the word God had given me. He had handed me the seed of a skill, and my job was to tend it faithfully, without knowing when it would bear fruit.

Again and again, God has spoken about my future before I could see even a hint of fulfillment. In nearly every major endeavor He's led me into, He has given me a word, and as I walked in obedience, I watched it unfold, always in His timing, never mine. Many of those seeds have taken years, even decades, to grow. Because of that, I've learned that faithfulness in the preparation season matters just as much as the fulfillment. When God speaks, I prepare. I wait. I keep tending the seed until He opens doors only He can open.

As I witnessed God work breakthrough after breakthrough, I had no idea He was about to move even bigger mountains in an area I had been told was completely impossible.

After college, I moved to Missouri, to my then-husband's hometown, and for years, I raised our family in the Midwest. Many parts were beautiful: strong church communities, wonderful schools for my children, and best friends who became family. I put down roots there, expecting to stay. Yet the distance from my own family in Virginia was costly. As one of nine children, I had always been shaped by the noise and nearness of home, but in that marriage, I grew increasingly isolated. Most years, I could visit family only once, sometimes not at all, and life kept happening without me. Weddings were celebrated, grandparents I adored grew frail and entered Glory, babies were born, holidays came and went, and I missed the ordinary moments that stitch a family together. The milestones piled up, and I was not there.

Despite this, when it came time to rebuild my life, I did not try to move out of Missouri. I didn't want to disrupt my children's lives any more than they already had been, and I truly valued the community we were in. I longed for a new normal with healthy co-parenting, predictable rhythms, and healing between my children and their father. My lawyers also cautioned me that in a state where fifty-fifty custody was standard, and I already held far more than that, relocation would be impossible. Not difficult, impossible. So, I settled in and concentrated on rebuilding life for my children and me.

During that time, my children were given the opportunity to attend summer youth camps with my praying church. Unable to afford the cost, the church generously provided partial scholarships for each of them. My oldest daughter was thrilled when her week arrived, especially since she was going with friends. Spiritually, she had fallen away from the Lord, so I prayed that camp would be a turning point. When she returned, she was overflowing with testimonies of how God met her there. Not only had she experienced a powerful outpouring of the Holy Spirit, but she was also given a prophetic word for our family: that we would be moving to Virginia.

I couldn't see how that could possibly happen. That word had not been given directly to me, but I told her I would pray and ask God to confirm it. And in time, He did. He gave me a very specific word in Scripture, one that seemed to surface everywhere I turned. Without knowing, people prayed it over me; it was prophesied to me, spoken to me, and appeared repeatedly in my quiet times. It was confirmed so often that my heart beat with belief that it was true. I kept praying boldly, "Lord, if this is Your word, make a way."

It wasn't just my heart that God began to prepare. He readied my children, too. I would not have considered moving if they were not on board, but even with understandable uncertainties, they were in full support.

Even though everything looked impossible, I started to prepare. Preparation is faith in practice. I began getting ready to move, trusting God to fulfill His promise. I asked family and friends to pray that God would move this mountain, and when I doubted, I looked at my Ebenezers. I consulted my lawyer and gathered every document she would need, even as she reminded me that courts almost never allowed relocation, especially out of state. I knew that was true, yet I also knew God, and if it was His will, He would make a way.

So, I earnestly prepared. I researched schools in Virginia and affordable places to live. I prepped my house to sell, making repairs and letting go of things we no longer needed. I researched moving companies and made sure my van could withstand a cross-country trip.

If it sounds like this time of preparation was smooth obedience, untouched by trouble, that would be disingenuous. It was a season of turmoil and exhaustion, both from stress and trials from my children's father and from the relentless physical pain I was enduring. But one truth had been hammered into my heart: if I fixed my eyes on the problems, I was overwhelmed. If I fixed my eyes on the promise, I saw God everywhere. My circumstances screamed "impossible," but my Ebenezers whispered, "Watch Him." Bold prayer calmed my heart when circumstances felt intimidating.

Many around me supported the promise I was clinging to, but a few tried to offer a "realistic" dose of discouragement. That did not dissuade me. I wasn't being careless; I was choosing to believe beyond my limited vision and borrow strength from God's.

By the time the court date requesting relocation came, my confidence was not in myself or my ability to persuade, but in the God who parts seas. This is where the story of the Israelites meets ours: a people asked to prepare for freedom before they could see the road, to pack by faith, to step toward a sea that had not yet split. As God led Israel out of Egypt, He showed us what it looks like to get ready for a promise while the waters are still calm.

When God set Israel on the path out of Egypt, He didn't start with the sea parting. He started with instructions. "This month is to be for you the first month," He said, resetting their calendar around His promise. He taught them how to eat a hurried meal, pack their bags, and mark their homes with the blood of a lamb (Exodus 12:2, NIV). It looked ordinary, but it was obedience that made room for deliverance. They were told to eat "with your cloak tucked into your belt, your sandals on your feet and your staff in your hand" (Exodus 12:11, NIV). In other words, be ready to move. Preparation was worship. Packing was faith in practice.

Then came the moment none of them could have engineered. With Pharaoh's army behind them and the Red Sea in front, the promise still stood, but the pathway looked impossible. Moses answered their panic with a word that has steadied me many times: "Do not be afraid. Stand firm and you will see the deliverance the Lord will bring you today" (Exodus 14:13, NIV). Then came the command: "Tell the Israelites to move on" (Exodus 14:15, NIV). God split the sea, but they still had to walk. Dry ground appears beneath obedient feet.

Their preparation did not end at the shoreline. In the wilderness, God trained them to live by promise rather than panic. He taught them to gather manna for today and trust Him for tomorrow, just as we see in Exodus 16:4–5. He led them with cloud and fire, as described in Exodus 13:21–22. He turned bitter water sweet and called them to remember His faithfulness (see Exodus 15:22–25). Every step was a lesson: keep moving, keep trusting, keep praying boldly, keep preparing.

That pattern has sculpted how I prepare, too. I cannot part seas, but I can put my shoes on. I can gather documents, make lists, pack boxes, and guard my heart from discouragement. I can move when God says "go" and wait in peace when He says "hold." Preparation does not make the miracle happen, but it makes me ready to walk when it does.

So while we waited for the court date, I kept taking the next obedient step. I prayed, I packed slowly, I researched schools, I kept a journal of confirmations, and I asked God to bring peace to my children's hearts. When fear tried to dominate, I returned to Israel at the water's edge and prayed, "Lord, help me stand firm in what You have said, and when You speak, help me move."

If you are holding a promise with no bridge in sight, take courage. Set your table with obedience. Eat with your sandals on. Write down what God has spoken so you can return to it when feelings try to drown it out. Ask for daily bread. Gather what He provides. Leave tomorrow in His hands. The God who marked Israel's doorposts knows yours, too. Pray boldly in the pain, and prepare as if the sea will split, because with Him, it can.

And God did it. Despite every voice that said relocation was impossible, the court released us to go. We packed the boxes we had been quietly preparing, scheduled the moving truck, loaded my beloved van, and drove east. In less than two weeks, because we had prepared, we moved halfway across the country to rebuild our lives. We reclaimed Virginia as home, the place I grew up, and the place God had been pointing our hearts. "The Lord has done great things for us, and we are filled with joy" (Psalm 126:3, NIV). What once felt like the Red Sea on every side became dry ground under our feet. He spoke, we prepared, He opened the way, and we walked through.

If you are holding a promise that seems far off, let this be a reminder: "The one who calls you is faithful, and he will do it" (1 Thessalonians 5:24, NIV). He will do it in His time and His way. Prepare what you can, trust Him with what you cannot, and be ready to move when He says move. Bold prayer, accompanied by obedient preparation, produces powerful results.

A Rescue Prayer

Dear God,

My heart is tired of waiting. I feel the weight of promises that seem distant and doors that will not open. Part of me wants to stop hoping so I won't be disappointed again. I wonder if I misheard You or if I am somehow disqualified. You see where I feel stuck, the fears that whisper "impossible," and the grief of delay. I bring all of it to You now.

But You are the God who fulfills every word You speak. You made a way through the sea, remembered Hannah, and fulfilled Your promise to Mary in Your perfect time. You do not forget Your children. Strengthen my faith to believe that what I cannot see, You are already working. Teach me to trust Your character when circumstances say otherwise.

So I choose to prepare, even while I wait. Show me the next faithful step and give me courage to obey. Give me peace when You say "not yet." Let my waiting become worship and my prayers a declaration of trust. I believe that You are faithful and that You will finish what You have begun.

In Jesus' name, I pray. Amen.

“The Spirit you received brought about your adoption to sonship. And by him we cry, ‘Abba, Father.’”

Romans 8:15 (NIV)

CHAPTER

Ten

When You Forget Who You Are

Sometimes life batters you back and forth until you forget who you are and, even more importantly, whose you are. Have you ever felt unworthy of all that God has for you? Even after you have watched Him answer prayers, it can still feel hard to ask for more. The enemy works to create distance between God and you, stirring shame, insecurity, and a sense that you are disqualified. So you step back from the very presence that heals you.

I had undeniably seen God move in my life, and yet I wrestled here. Safely nestled in Virginia, my children and I were still recovering. We felt safer, but uncertainty lingered. God kept doing a new thing in me, healing, restoring, refining, even as fresh challenges surfaced. I was off prescription medications, yet pain still flared. Even so, I had watched my capacity grow.

As I tended to physical and emotional healing after a destructive marriage, my body slowly began to recognize safety. Muscles that had been locked in tension for years began, little by little, to release. It did not happen overnight. It has taken years of prioritizing healing.

He is continuing His work of healing in my body, but the pain that once screamed has quieted to a background hum. It still spikes at times, and when it does, I remember how far God has brought me. Strength continues to return. Where pain once colored every moment, now you would only know it was there if I told you. Where I once could not raise my left arm in worship, every time I lift it now I am declaring that God has defeated the enemy. He is healing my body, restoring what felt lost, and turning weakness into a living testimony of His power.

For years in my marriage, my value felt measured by what I could do, how quiet and careful I became so I would not trigger anger, and how well I could disappear into myself to keep the peace. I learned to mute my needs, to live contained, and to tiptoe through each day so I would not upset anything. Over time, that distorted the way I saw myself. I did not just feel unloved. I felt unworthy of being loved. And when you carry that long enough, you begin to come to God the same way, wondering if you are too much, not enough, or somehow disqualified from what He gives so freely.

Maybe you know that feeling. Maybe someone's words, neglect, betrayal, or constant criticism have become the mirror you hold up to your soul: a parent whose approval you never quite earned, a spouse who withheld tenderness, a church leader who dismissed your voice, or a boss who treated you as replaceable. After a while, you begin to assume God must see you the same way: barely acceptable, barely tolerable, barely wanted.

Even with so much healing, I still found myself running to the altar, asking for God's best, while a quiet voice whispered, "Maybe you have already been given too much to ask for more. Maybe you do not deserve what you have." When that happens, prayer pulls inward and shrinks, shaped more by what you fear than by what the Father delights to give His children. You approach God cautiously, almost as if you are unsure whether you are truly welcome.

But Scripture tells a different story. God does not start with what disqualifies you. He starts with what He has already declared: "Do not fear, for I have redeemed you; I have summoned you by name; you are mine" (Isaiah 43:1, NIV). Before you list your failures, He says, "You belong to Me."

Before Jesus went to the cross, He made a promise that changes how you see yourself and how you pray. He told His disciples that those who believe in Him would continue His work and even see greater works through His Spirit, because He was going to the Father. He taught that when you ask in His name, it is for the Father's glory (John 14:12–17, NIV). He was preparing them, and you, for a new kind of access to God. This access is not through a building or a human priest. It is made possible because the Holy Spirit dwells within ordinary people like you.

The cross is what made that access possible. Humanity's sin had created a gap that no effort, goodness, or religion could cross. The law required a perfect sacrifice, and Jesus became that sacrifice, the One who bore your punishment so you could be made whole (Hebrews 9:22; Isaiah 53:5, NIV). His death was not an accident. It was God's rescue plan.

When Jesus died, the curtain in the temple that separated the Most Holy Place from everyone else was torn in two from top to bottom (Matthew 27:51, NIV). God Himself did that, showing that the barrier between you and His presence had been removed.

For generations, only the high priest could cross that curtain, and only once a year, with fear and elaborate preparation. Now, because of Jesus, access is no longer restricted. You do not come to God carrying your own worth. You come carrying the worth He placed on you when Jesus gave His life to bring you near.

After His resurrection, Jesus appeared to His disciples who were hiding behind locked doors, afraid and ashamed. They had run from Him in His darkest hour. Yet He came to them with peace, not condemnation, and then did something remarkable. He breathed on them and said, "Receive the Holy Spirit" (John 20:21–22, NRSV).

Just as God once breathed life into Adam, Jesus breathed new spiritual life into His followers. This was not just comfort. It was a declaration: "You are not forsaken. You are not alone. My Spirit lives in you."

Because of Jesus' finished work, Scripture says you are justified, declared righteous by faith. "Since we are justified by faith, we have peace with God through our Lord Jesus Christ" (Romans 5:1, NRSV). Peace with God is not a feeling. It is a settled reality. The battle is over. The distance is closed. You do not have to earn your way back into His favor every day.

And that is why your identity is adoption, not audition.

The Bible says you have received "the Spirit of adoption," and by that Spirit you cry, "Abba, Father" (Romans 8:15, NRSV). This is the language of closeness, not formality. In Christ, you are chosen, named, and welcomed. Children who know they belong ask differently. They come close. They do not hover at the doorway, afraid they will be turned away.

So when Hebrews invites you to "approach the throne of grace with confidence" to receive mercy and find grace to help you in your time of need (Hebrews 4:16, NIV), it is not telling you to be brash. It is telling you to live like who you are. You are not an outsider hoping for a spare blessing. You are a child of a generous Father who delights to give good gifts to those He loves.

Sometimes, though, it is easier to believe this for other people than for ourselves. For years, I prayed my closest friends would see themselves through God's eyes instead of through the fog of damaged self-image. I knew that if they glimpsed who He says they are, it would change everything. Then one day, I realized I had never truly prayed that for myself.

Years in a destructive marriage had warped the way I saw my own reflection. I could say "God loves me" with my mouth, but deep down I felt like the girl forgotten in the corner of the room, trying not to bother anyone, grateful for scraps. The enemy's lies had slowly replaced the image God had given. So I started asking simply, "God, let me see myself through Your eyes."

Slowly, my vision changed. Not all at once, but piece by piece. I began to realize that I am a child of the King. He made me. He chose me. He sees every imperfect part and still delights in me. Scripture gave me language for that reality: the Father has lavished His love on us by calling us His children, and that is who we are (1 John 3:1). In love, He planned, long before I was born, to adopt me into His family through Jesus (Ephesians 1:4–5). And because I am in Christ, there is now no condemnation over my life (Romans 8:1, NIV).

The more I agreed with what God said, the quieter the old lies became. I stopped praying like an outsider and started praying like a daughter who already belongs there. When shame tried to silence my requests, I remembered that the God who did not spare His own Son will also graciously give us what we truly need (Romans 8:32). If He already paid the highest price to bring me close, He is not looking for reasons to push me away.

Practically, this meant answering lies with truth in real time. When that old internal voice said, "You are too much. You are not enough. You should be quieter. You should not speak up. You do not deserve kindness. You are not worthy of good things. You should be better by now," I began to answer with what God has named me: chosen, holy, and dearly loved (Colossians 3:12). I stopped bargaining for access and instead called, "Abba, Father." I pictured the throne of grace as an open door and, by faith, walked toward it on purpose, trusting I would find mercy and help right when I needed it. I also started marking every trace of healing with gratitude. Each time my nerve-damaged left arm lifts in worship, it is not just a movement. It is a flag planted. God is winning ground in me.

Seeing yourself as God sees you may not make life easier, but it will anchor you. Identity does not just change how you see yourself. It changes how you approach God.

Because of who you are in Christ, the way you pray changes.

Come to God with confidence. You are not barely tolerated. You are invited. Scripture makes this clear: you are to approach His throne of grace with confidence so that you may receive mercy and find grace to help you in your time of need (Hebrews 4:16, NIV). Your welcome is not based on how well you performed this week. It is based on Jesus.

Pray in the authority of the mighty name of Jesus. Scripture says that when you ask in His name, the Father is glorified in the Son (John 14:13–14, NIV). You are not standing on your own merit. You are standing in His authority, backed by His power and presence.

Ask for what only God can do. Do not limit your prayers to what you can understand or manage. God is able to do immeasurably more than all you ask or imagine (Ephesians 3:20–21, NIV). Bring Him what feels impossible and trust Him with the outcome.

Align your prayers with what God has already said. Jesus taught that faith can speak to mountains and see them move (Mark 11:23–24, NIV). Bold prayer agrees with God before circumstances change.

Pray the nature and character of God over each situation. Pray for justice because He is just. Pray for healing because He is a healer. Pray for restoration because He restores. Pray for deliverance because He is a deliverer. Pray His names and His nature over each situation.

Pray with faith, even when doubt is present. Scripture is clear that when you ask, you are to believe and not doubt (James 1:6–7, NIV). Faith does not mean you have no questions. It means your questions do not keep you from coming. Pray when you doubt, knowing that He is faithful.

Worship while you are waiting. Throughout Scripture, God's people worshiped before they saw the outcome (2 Chronicles 20:21–22, NIV). Worship fixes your attention on who God is instead of what you are facing. Praise Him for what He will do in your situation.

Keep praying. Do not stop because something takes time. Jesus taught that you should always pray and not give up (Luke 18:1, NIV). Persistence is not pressure on God. It is trust in Him. Do not stop seeking, knocking, and asking. God honors persistent prayer.

Pray when you do not have the words. When you do not know what to pray, you are not alone. The Holy Spirit Himself intercedes for you (Romans 8:26, NIV). He is at work even when you do not have the words.

This is what it looks like to pray boldly.

We do not pray as those trying to get God's attention. We pray as His children. Because of Christ's finished work, the Spirit within us, and the Father who has already claimed us, we are invited to come to Him with confidence.

So when you forget who you are, remember this: you belong to Him. Come to Him boldly.

A Rescue Prayer

Dear God,

I feel the weight of old lies trying to pull me back into insecurity and shame. There are moments when I forget who I am and start to question what I am allowed to ask of You. I hesitate in prayer, wondering if I am asking for too much or if I am even worthy to come. My heart feels small, and my confidence feels shaken.

But You have already declared what is true. You have called me by name, and I belong to You. Because of Jesus, I am not on the outside trying to earn my way in. I am Your child, welcomed into Your presence. You are a good Father who hears me, receives me, and invites me to come with confidence.

So I will come to You boldly. I will not hold back my prayers or shrink my requests. I will trust Your Word, believe in Your power, and continue to come, even when I don't understand. Teach me to pray with faith, to worship while I wait, and to rest in the truth that I belong to You.

In Jesus' name, I pray. Amen.

"Let us then approach God's throne of grace with confidence, so that we may receive mercy and find grace to help us in our time of need."

Hebrews 4:16 (NIV)

CHAPTER

Eleven

When You Step into Bold Faith

You've walked through some deep places on these pages: pain that persists, doubt in God's goodness, trust that feels shaky, grief that robs your breath, and seasons where you have needed a breakthrough and could not make it happen on your own. You have heard stories of God's faithfulness and remembered some of your own. You have been invited to bring more of your heart into God's presence instead of trying to hold it together alone.

And yet, as you come to this chapter, many things may still be unresolved. Some prayers have not been answered the way you hoped. Some wounds are still tender. Some situations look exactly the same on the outside. It can be hard to imagine praying boldly when you feel worn out, disappointed, or unsure. Bold prayer can sound like something reserved for people who feel strong, certain, and victorious.

But that is not who God waits for.

Throughout Scripture, God meets people in the middle of their weakness and invites them to call on Him. Hannah prayed through tears. David worshiped and wept in caves and on battlefields. Job cried out through confusion and loss. The early church prayed while facing threats, pressure, and persecution. None of them waited until life felt perfect before they prayed. They brought the mess into the presence of God and found Him there.

Bold prayer is not pretending you are okay. Bold prayer is bringing your "not okay" to a God who is still completely faithful. It is telling the truth about how much it hurts, and then choosing to talk to Him anyway. It is saying, "Lord, this is more than I can handle, but it is not more than You can handle."

This kind of praying is not something you manufacture through willpower. It is something the Holy Spirit cultivates in you. The same Spirit who hovered over the waters at creation, who raised Jesus from the dead, who filled the early church with courage and power; that same Spirit draws near to you when you pray. He reminds you of what is true, strengthens you when you feel empty, and helps you pray even when you cannot find words.

If you belong to Jesus, the Holy Spirit lives in you. He is your Comforter, your Helper, your Advocate. He's the One who walks with you into doctors' offices, courtrooms, quiet bedrooms, and tearful nights. He calms what fear stirs up. He nudges you to forgive when bitterness starts to grow. He gives you wisdom that you know did not come from you. He prompts you to pray for someone out of the blue, and later you find out that was the very moment they needed it most. His presence is not just an idea; it is real help in real moments.

And if you are not sure you belong to Jesus yet, I want you to hear this clearly: God's heart toward you is open. He is not waiting for you to fix yourself before you come. Jesus came for you while you were still far from Him, still tangled in sin, still trying to carry life on your own. On the cross, He took the weight of your sin and shame, and in His resurrection, He opened the way for you to be forgiven, made new, and brought into God's family.

To belong to Jesus is not a matter of cleaning up your life and hoping God accepts you. It is surrendering to the One who has already done the saving work. If you sense Him drawing you, you don't have to have the right words. You don't have to pray these exact words, but if this reflects your heart, you can use it as a guide:

Jesus, I need You.

I confess that I have sinned and tried to live life my own way.

I believe You died for me and rose again.

I turn from my sin and trust You as my Savior and Lord.

Please forgive me, make me new, and fill me with Your Holy Spirit.

I give my life to You.

Those words are not a magic formula. What matters is the surrender of your heart. If you prayed that in faith, heaven rejoices, and your story has a new beginning. You are now a child of God, and the Holy Spirit has come to dwell in you, not as a visitor, but as the very presence of God living within you.

Whether you have walked with Jesus for many years or are just now considering what it means to trust Him, the invitation is the same: come close. Bring Him your heart. Bring Him your questions. Bring Him your pain. You do not have to hold back with God.

Because of Jesus, you have a standing invitation to come before the throne of grace with confidence, so you can receive mercy and find grace to help you in your time of need (Hebrews 4:16, NIV). That is not a suggestion for the days when you feel strong; it is a lifeline for the days when you feel weak. God does not grow tired of your voice. He is not rolling His eyes at another prayer. He hears and welcomes every cry and every whisper.

As you choose to pray in the middle of your pain, something begins to shift. You might not see change right away in your circumstances, but the Holy Spirit is at work in you. He soothes your heart. He reminds you of God's promises. He gives you the strength to move when you feel stuck. He pours

God's love into the places that feel empty, and He helps your prayers move from fear to trust.

Bold prayer is honest and expectant. It says, "Lord, here is where it hurts. Here is what I cannot fix. Here is what I long for. I know You see me, and I believe You are able." It asks for healing in broken bodies and broken hearts. It asks for justice in situations that feel unfair. It asks for provision in places where the numbers do not add up. It asks for hope when everything feels dark. It keeps asking, not to wear God down, but because it believes His heart is kind and His power is real.

As you step out of these pages and back into your own story, I do not want you to simply close this book and move on. I want you to walk forward with a deeper awareness that you are not alone. The God who met you as you read is the God who goes with you into whatever comes next. His Holy Spirit is not confined to church altars or special moments; He is present in your kitchen, your car, your office, your hospital room, your quiet evenings, and your noisy mornings.

So let this be a turning point. Not where you pretend the pain is gone, but where you decide you will not carry it by yourself. Not where you promise to be stronger, but where you invite Him to be your strength. Not where you try to control outcomes, but where you place your story into the hands of the One who loves you most.

If you have never given your life to Jesus and you sense Him drawing you, you can respond right now, in simple faith. If you have already trusted Him, you can still lift your heart and ask for more of His Spirit's work in you. Either way, you do not have to wait for a better moment or a better version of yourself. You can come as you are. Don't delay. He is waiting to welcome you.

If you have known Jesus for a long time but feel disillusioned or disheartened, this moment can be a fresh start for you as well. You can ask the Holy Spirit to fill you again, to renew your courage, to soften what has grown hard, and to set your heart back on fire for the things of God. You can step into the coming days with a quiet, steady confidence that the Lord is with you and for you.

So as you read this chapter, I want to speak a blessing over you:

May you know, deep in your bones, that you are loved by your Father in heaven. May you be freshly filled with an outpouring of the Holy Spirit; comforted, strengthened, led, and empowered to pray and live boldly. May your prayers grow more honest, more specific, and more expectant. May your heart be anchored in the character of God, even when you cannot see what He is doing. May boldness rise in you, not because you feel strong, but because He is strong in you.

You are not walking out of these pages empty-handed. You are walking forward with the Word of God in your heart, the Spirit of God within you, and an open invitation to come boldly before the God who loves you.

Keep talking to Him. Keep trusting Him. Keep asking Him to move. And watch, with a hopeful heart, for all the ways He will, because He will.

A Rescue Prayer

Dear God,

I come to You with a heart that feels both longing and hesitant. There are places in my life that still hurt, prayers that feel unfinished, and battles that have left me weary. I want to pray boldly, but pain makes me unsure, and fear tries to quiet my voice. I do not always feel strong or brave, but I bring my whole heart to You anyway. Meet me here in the places that feel tender and overwhelmed.

You are the God who sees me when I feel invisible. You are the Father who listens when I whisper my fears. You are the Savior who carries what I cannot. You are the Holy Spirit who strengthens me and intercedes when I have no words. You are faithful, powerful, and near. Because of who You are, I do not have to shrink back. I can come boldly before You.

So I choose to step forward in faith. Fill me with courage and expectation. Teach me to pray with honesty and confidence. Strengthen me for what is ahead. Revive what is weary and restore what is broken. I trust that You are at work and that You will lead me faithfully.

In Jesus' name, I pray. Amen.

"He who began a good work in you will carry it on to completion until the day of Christ Jesus."

Philippians 1:6 (NIV)

CHAPTER

Twelve

When God Writes the Ending

When I look back over my life, I don't see a perfect story or a carefully managed plan. I see the mercy of God. I see a Father who kept pursuing me through seasons of joy and seasons of devastation. I see Jesus, present in both the victories and the valleys. I see the Holy Spirit, steady and faithful, leading me gently one small step at a time when I could not see more than the very next thing.

If there is anything beautiful, fruitful, or noteworthy in my life, it is because the Lord has done it. Scripture says, "Let the one who boasts boast in the Lord" (1 Corinthians 1:31, NIV). That is what is worth sharing, a testimony of what He has done, so that your confidence will rest in His power, not in mine.

Professionally, God has written a story I never could have imagined. That first unexpected $200 writing job came from a publishing executive I had barely spoken with in twenty years, Tom Freiling. I did not know it then, but God was using that reconnection to redirect the entire course of my life. Tom became a mentor, a boss, and eventually a trusted publishing partner as we co-created *Rescue Prayers*. What began as one small assignment grew into steady ghostwriting, then into the work of an editorial director, and eventually into helping authors steward the messages God had entrusted to them. One project led to another until I suddenly realized I was working full-time in publishing, the very field I had once only dreamed about. Every open door, every opportunity, every platform has been the Lord's goodness at work.

In time, God further opened the door for me to serve as vice president of the publishing company, to help create books that now sit on shelves at places like Barnes & Noble, and to come alongside leaders whose messages carry hope and healing. He allowed me to write best-selling books under my own name and to quietly help sculpt many others behind the scenes. Some of my books have been featured on the radio, local news, and national networks such as NBC, CBS, ABC, and FOX. Many have received endorsements from New York Times best-selling authors and respected public figures. None of that feels like a personal achievement; it feels like grace. God took a gift that once felt buried under years of pain and breathed on it so that it could serve His purposes.

He has also given me the privilege of speaking, both in ministry settings and in the professional world. I have spoken at churches, conferences, retreats, leadership gatherings, publishing seminars, Bible studies, and events where people come hungry either for God's presence or for practical training that helps them steward their own calling. Whether I am teaching Scripture, encouraging those who are walking through hardship, or equipping writers and leaders to communicate with greater clarity and impact, I count it a sacred blessing. I feel God's pleasure when He speaks through me.

Standing before a room, whether a sanctuary, a conference hall, or a boardroom, and watching the Holy Spirit minister in ways no human could orchestrate remains one of the greatest honors of my life. I pray the Lord continues to open doors for me to teach, speak, and pour into others, because my deepest desire is to point people back to the goodness, wisdom, and nearness of Jesus in every space He allows me to serve. I never want to stop testifying to what He has done or sharing biblical truth that helps set others free.

My story is not mine; it is definitively His. The Lord ministered to me when chronic pain tormented my days and nights. He upheld me when I could barely stand. He brought real healing to my body, calming symptoms that once defined my life, and I trust Him as my Healer to finish what He has started. I move and live and serve in a strength that only He could have restored. He has carried me through divorce, courtrooms, financial strain, parenting storms, and deep grief. He has guarded my children, provided in ways that even I cannot understand, and gently rebuilt my heart where it had been shattered. The victories I walk in now are not evidence of my resilience; they are evidence of His enduring faithfulness.

One of the greatest gifts He has given me is the privilege of praying with others, as His boldness in me has empowered me to speak prayers only He can fulfill, again and again, over countless lives.

I have prayed in church sanctuaries and at crowded altars, but I have just as often prayed in ordinary and unexpected places. I have prayed with strangers in busy hair salons, with servers in restaurants, with women in church bathrooms, with friends in parking lots, and with parents on the sidelines of sporting events. I have prayed in hospital rooms and waiting areas, in quiet corners at conferences, and during late-night phone calls when someone's world was falling apart. I have knelt in living rooms, held hands in kitchens, whispered prayers in hallways, and lifted my voice in the Hall of Heroes at the Pentagon. I have prayed in emails, text messages, and long conversations where I could not physically be present, but God could.

Every one of those moments has felt holy because of the power of the Holy Spirit at work.

Why am I so passionate about prayer? I pray with urgency because I know God answers. I have watched Him answer in my own life too many times to stay quiet when someone else is in need. I have seen Him heal bodies, soften hearts, open doors, restore relationships, give wisdom, stabilize emotions, and provide in ways that were clearly His doing. When someone asks, "Will you pray?" my heart's response is immediate: "Of course. Let's bring this to the One who can actually do something about it."

That posture is at the heart of what eventually became *Rescue Prayers.*

Over time, I realized how many people longed to pray but felt like they did not have the words. In seasons of deep grief, depression, anxiety, pain, illness, or overwhelming circumstances, sometimes we do not even have the energy or emotional capacity to form a single sentence. People would tell me they believed God was real, but the moment they tried to pray, all they felt was numb, blank, or stuck. I recognized that feeling because I had lived it. There were seasons when I sat in silence with a heart full of need and very few words to offer.

In that tension, the Holy Spirit began to nudge my heart: "Give them prayers they can borrow until their own voice returns."

Rescue Prayers began as an offering for weary people who did not know how to talk to God about what they were walking through. Each prayer was crafted to sit beside them in the pain, to help hold up their arms when they were tired, and to lead their hearts back into the presence of a God who loves them. I wrote out of my own battles and the comfort I had received, not to center my story, but to say, "Here. If you can't find words right now, use these. Let this be a starting place."

These prayers were never meant to replace the work of the Holy Spirit. Scripture tells us that even when we do not know what to pray, the Spirit Himself intercedes for us with groanings too deep for words. *Rescue Prayers* simply lend language that helps you agree with what He is already doing in your heart and already praying over your life.

What I did not expect was the scope of what God would do with that simple yes. *Rescue Prayers* has allowed me to "pray with" people I will never meet this side of heaven, people who read a prayer at 2:00 a.m. and feel less alone, people who keep a book by their hospital bed, people who send specific prayers to friends walking through grief, depression, anxiety, chronic pain, or cancer. It has connected me with pastors, counselors, chaplains, and ministry leaders who use these prayers as tools to help others draw near to God when life is hard.

None of this was something I engineered. It was God, taking the places where He rescued me and turning them into lifelines for others.

So, as I "boast" in this chapter, here is what I am really boasting in. I boast in the Lord who took a girl who loved words and grew her into a writer, editor, and publishing leader for His purposes. I boast in the Lord who met a broken, exhausted mom and restored her body, renewed her mind, and placed a fresh fire in her heart for His presence. I boast in the Lord who allowed me to see His power in my own life so that when I pray with others, I can say with confidence, "I know He hears you. I have watched Him move." I boast in the Lord who took my pain, my questions, my Ebenezers, and my yes, and turned them into prayers that now reach far beyond what I could ever touch on my own. And I boast in the Lord who continues to pour out His goodness over our *Rescue Prayers* family, answering prayers in hospital rooms, homes, church pews, quiet cars, and tearful late nights, showing that He is still near and still faithful.

If you hold this book in your hands, it is because God answers prayer. He answered mine in ways I never could have imagined, and I believe with all my heart that He will answer yours as well, in the way His wisdom and love know is best. His answers do not always look the way we expect or arrive on the timeline we prefer, but they always come wrapped in His great love and unwavering faithfulness.

My life is not tidy or pain-free. I still face difficult days full of lingering questions and places where I am waiting on God to move. But over all of it stands this truth: He is faithful. His character is perfect, even when my circumstances are not. He has not answered every prayer the way I once envisioned, yet He has never ignored a single cry. Time and again, He has met me with exactly what I needed, sometimes rescue, sometimes strength, sometimes a miraculous yes, sometimes a loving "not yet," but always Himself.

The same God who opened doors for me can open doors for you. The same God who healed the parts of me I thought were permanently broken can bring healing to your story. The same God who taught me to pray with bold trust will teach you to pray that way, too.

And here is what I do not want you to miss: God delights in answering prayer, and He invites you to ask. Scripture says, "You do not have because you do not ask God" (James 4:2, NIV). That is not a rebuke; it is an invitation into a relationship. Your Father is not distant or indifferent. His ear is inclined toward you. He longs to meet you in the very places that ache the most, and He calls you to bring them to Him.

As we reach the end of these pages, my prayer is that this will not feel like the close of a book, but the beginning, or the deepening, of a life marked by honest, Spirit-led, courageous prayer. When life is painful, you do not have to pull back. You can come into the presence of God with a pain-filled heart and say, "Here is where it hurts. Here is what I cannot fix. Here is what I am asking You to do."

Keep talking to Him. Keep trusting His heart. Keep presenting your needs before Him with expectation. You do not pray because your faith is flawless, but because His faithfulness is. You do not pray because you have everything under control, but because He holds all things together. You do not pray because you are strong, but because His strength meets you in your weakness.

This entire book has been my humble offering to say: God still answers. He answered me in moments of deep sorrow and in days overflowing with joy. And He will answer you, faithfully and personally, according to His perfect wisdom. His way may surprise you. His timing may stretch you. But every prayer entrusted to Him is seen, treasured, and held.

So bring Him your pain. Bring Him your fear. Bring Him your longing and your hope. Pray boldly when life is painful, and then watch, with a heart turned toward Him, for all the ways He will move, because He always is.

He is the Author who writes beginnings and endings. He is the Healer who restores what feels lost. He is the Provider who meets your needs with tenderness and wisdom. He is the One who answers.

And He is not finished with you yet.

A Rescue Prayer

Dear God,

I come to You with an open heart. Some places in my life still feel tender and unresolved, but I trust that You are not finished with me. Thank You for meeting me in my pain, for hearing every prayer I have prayed, and for reminding me that Your presence remains steady even when my circumstances do not. I believe You see me, You love me, and You are still at work.

Lord, pour out boldness in me by Your Spirit. Strengthen my faith where it feels weak and renew hope where it has grown quiet. Anchor my heart in who You are so I can pray with confidence, not because I feel strong, but because You are faithful. Teach me to come to You honestly and expectantly. Guide me and give me courage to keep praying in every season.

Thank You for being the God who answers. I surrender my life into Your hands. Heal what is wounded, restore what has been lost, and provide what I need. Fill my life with peace, strength, and expectation. I trust that You will be faithful, and I will watch for the ways You move.

In Jesus' name, I pray. Amen.

About the Author

Christen M. Jeschke is the author of the best-selling Rescue Prayers series, prayer books written to help people find words to talk to God in life's hardest moments.

A fourth-generation pastor's daughter, Christen has spent more than twenty years in ministry and is passionate about helping people encounter God through prayer and His Word.

What Christen teaches is rooted in personal experience. Having walked through seasons that tested her faith and reshaped her understanding of God's presence, she writes with a deep conviction about what it means to continue seeking Him when answers feel delayed and faith feels costly.

Her books have been widely shared and gifted to those walking through grief, illness, anxiety, and seasons of deep uncertainty. Her work has been featured across national media outlets including NBC, ABC, FOX, and CBS News, and has appeared in Barnes & Noble and major retailers worldwide. She serves as Vice President at Freiling Agency, where she works with authors to develop and publish messages that carry lasting impact.

Through both writing and speaking, Christen communicates biblical truth with clarity, depth, and conviction. She always returns to the same unchanging reality: God is present, He is faithful, and He invites us to come to Him boldly.

Prayers Answered: Praying Boldly When Life Is Painful is an invitation to move beyond hesitant prayer and approach God with the confidence of a child who knows their Father is listening. For those who have wrestled with silence, doubt, or discouragement in their prayer life, this book offers a steady reminder that God hears, God responds, and He remains at work.

Christen lives in Virginia with her children.

About Rescue Prayers

Rescue Prayers was created for moments when life feels overwhelming and it is hard to find the words to pray. In seasons of grief, anxiety, illness, or uncertainty, these prayers are designed to help you come before God honestly, even when your heart feels heavy and your thoughts feel scattered.

Each prayer follows a simple, powerful pattern inspired by the Psalms: a place to cry out, a reminder of who God is, and a declaration of trust in what He will do. You are invited to bring your real emotions before Him, to remember His faithfulness, and to rest in the truth that He is greater than whatever you are facing.

You do not have to carry this alone. God sees you, He hears you, and He is present in your situation. Even when answers feel delayed or circumstances feel too heavy, He is actively working in your life right now, even in ways you cannot yet see.

Scan the QR code below to explore more Rescue Prayers, find encouragement for your current season, and receive ongoing support as you continue to seek God in prayer.

Scan to explore more at RescuePrayers.com

www.ingramcontent.com/pod-product-compliance
Lightning Source LLC
LaVergne TN
LVHW051008080826
845145LV00009B/2509

* 9 7 8 1 9 6 9 8 2 6 4 9 8 *